Cambridge Studies in Social and Cultural Anthropology

99

THE ARCHITECTURE OF MEMORY

Recalling life in a single house that was occupied by several Jewish and Muslim families in the generation before Algeria's independence, Joëlle Bahloul's informants build up a multi-vocal micro-history of a way of life which came to an end in the early 1960s. Uprooted and dispersed, these former neighbours constantly refer back to the architecture of the house itself, which, with its internal boundaries and shared spaces, structures their memories. Here, in miniature, is a domestic history of North African Muslims, Jews, and Christians, living under French colonial rule.

Cambridge Studies in Social and Cultural Anthropology

The monograph series Cambridge Studies in Social and Cultural Anthropology publishes analytical ethnographies, comparative works, and contributions to theory. All combine an expert and critical command of ethnography and a sophisticated engagement with current theoretical debates.

A list of books in the series will be found at the end of the volume.

THE ARCHITECTURE OF MEMORY

A Jewish–Muslim household in colonial Algeria, 1937–1962

JOËLLE BAHLOUL
Indiana University

TRANSLATED FROM THE FRENCH BY CATHERINE DU PELOUX MÉNAGÉ

CAMBRIDGE
UNIVERSITY PRESS

Published by the Press Syndicate of the University of Cambridge
The Pitt Building, Trumpington Street, Cambridge CB2 1RP
40 West 20th Street, New York, NY 10011-4211, USA
10 Stamford Road, Oakleigh, Melbourne 3166, Australia
and Editions de la Maison des Sciences de l'Homme
54 Boulevard Raspail, 75270 Paris Cedex 06

Originally published in French as *La maison de mémoire*
by Editions Anne-Marie Métailié 1992
and © Editions Anne-Marie Métailié

First published in English by Editions de la Maison des Sciences de l'Homme and
Cambridge University Press 1996 as *The architecture of memory: a Jewish–Muslim
household in colonial Algeria, 1937–1962*
English translation © Maison des Sciences de l'Homme and
Cambridge University Press 1996

Printed in Great Britain at the University Press, Cambridge

A catalogue record for this book is available from the British Library

A catalogue record for this book is available from the Library of Congress

ISBN 0 521 41891 7 hardback
ISBN 0 521 56892 7 paperback
ISBN 2 7351 0689 6 hardback (France only)
ISBN 2 7351 0690 X paperback (France only)

SE

This book is dedicated to the
memory of Reine and Braham F.,
my grandparents,

and to everyone who lived
in D.A., regardless of gender, age, or religion.

Not only our memories but the things we have forgotten are 'housed'. Our soul is an abode. And by remembering 'houses' and 'rooms', we learn to 'abide' within ourselves.　　　　　　Gaston Bachelard, *The Poetics of Space*

Contents

Figures

Chronology

1958   Departure of the Bakoushe family for the Rue d'Aumale; Charlie
       Senoussi's wedding in Constantine; Eddie and Clarisse's departure
       for Algiers.

1959   Establishment of a local radio station in Sétif; sale of the
       Senoussis' butcher shop; bar mitzvah of Benjamin Senoussi.

1960   Deaths of Moushi Senoussi in March and of Polo Bakoushe in
       April; Benjamin Senoussi leaves school at age fourteen.

1961   Departure of the Bakoushe family for France; departure of the last
       Senoussi for Algiers.

1962   Departure of the Senoussis for France.

Acknowledgements

Writing this book has not been entirely an intimate, solitary project. All along, I have been inhabited by others' voices. A number of people have contributed, in one way or another, to the writing. My own contribution is a tribute to all my relatives, to my parents, to Maurice, Rolande, Georges, Eliane, Jacqueline, Yvon, André, Gilbert, Nelly, Clémence, Annie, Zerdoude, Jacky, Gérard, Renée, La Petite Souda, Marlène, Gisèle, Roger, and to Yolande and Raymond G., to Hocine, Zoubida, Saliha, Shelbiya, and Zohra. I also want to pay special tribute to the memory of Reinette, who died before the book was published, leaving behind her moving testimony. All these people's words are a lesson in humanity.

I am indebted to several colleagues and friends for their intellectual and personal support. I thank Michael Herzfeld, Michael Jackson, Annie Kriegel, and Jacques Hassoun. My Cambridge University Press editor, Jessica Kuper, and the press's reviewers have my gratitude for their support and thoughtful suggestions, Barbara Metzger for her help in improving the English version, and Catherine Ménagé for her translation. The whole project would have been much poorer without the encouragement of my husband, Marshall Leaffer, whose questions, comments, and patient review of my writing have gently enriched my experience of this book. Finally, I thank the Centre National de la Recherche Scientifique and the Ecole des Hautes Etudes en Sciences Sociales (Paris) for funding my ethnographic fieldwork in Algeria and the Maurice Amado Foundation for funding the translation.

Glossary

This glossary contains terms belonging to the Arabic spoken by Sétif's Jews (A) and Hebrew (H). The latter is mainly used to designate religious rituals, prayers, and liturgical objects. In the transcription of these terms *sh* represents the English *sh*, *h* the aspirate *h*, *kh* the guttural *h*, and *q* the guttural *k*.

'ada (A)	custom
ahrissa (A)	purée of ground red chilli peppers preserved in oil
b'dikat-hames (H)	pre-Passover verification of the absence of fermented substances in the house
brith mila (H)	circumcision
dar- (A)	house
dhimmis (A)	non-Muslim communities under Muslim law
djare (A)	tomato and garlic soup with mint
djinn (pl. *djnoun*) (A)	evil spirit
douwar (A)	countryside or rural community
el-braydji (A)	the man from Bordj-Bou-Arreridj or the countryman
el-haffef (A)	the hairdresser
'ers (A)	festive appearance
gandoura (A)	robe worn by Arab women under the veil
goy (H)	non-Jew
hallah (H)	bread baked on sabbath or on major religious holidays

hames (H)	fermented food forbidden for consumption during Passover
hammam (A)	public bath
hamos (A)	chick-pea
hanoukiya (H)	an eight-candle candelabrum used for Hanukkah
hart- (A)	courtyard, district
hatan (H)	bridegroom
hayik (A)	woollen blanket
haze, zeze (A)	eldest brother (form of address)
kanoun (A)	three-legged brazier made of clay
ka'ak (A)	crown-shaped cookie
kesa'a (A)	copper basin used for washing
kesra (A)	non-fermented grilled flat bread
kowedj (A)	baker or owner of the collective oven
lala (A)	eldest sister (form of address)
makrud (A)	fried cookie made of semolina and stuffed with dates
mektub (A)	destiny (written in God's records)
meqsofa (A)	impudent girl
metlo'h (A)	grilled leavened flat bread
mimuna (A)	celebration of the end of Passover
miqve (H)	Jewish ritual bath
mitzvah or *misva* (H)	observance of a divine commandment
m'ketfa (A)	blocked
m'khater (A)	soupy stew made of lamb with eggs
oulad-rumiya or *-romiya* (A)	children of a Christian woman
qowem (A)	ritual showing of the bride's trousseau
romiya (A)	Christian (or Catholic) woman (masc. *romi*)
rwama (A)	masculine plural form of *romi*, the Christians
salha (A)	therapeutic session to cure a person possessed by devils
shorba (A)	spicy tomato soup
sôl (A)	festive atmosphere
tabona (A)	three-legged brazier larger than a *kanoun*
tadjin (A)	round earthenware dish or board to broil flat bread; also, stew cooked in this dish
teba (H)	rabbi's pulpit in the synagogue

t'fina (A)	thick stew cooked slowly overnight and eaten for sabbath lunch
tsh'ha (A)	grotesque character in popular Jewish folk-tales of the Maghreb
tshuktshuka (A)	salad of sautéed tomatoes and peppers
yehud (A)	Jew (pl. *yehudin*); may be an insult in everyday Arabic
youyou (A)	ululation

Introduction: the ethnologist and her double

The idea of writing this book struck me all of a sudden in the spring of 1979. I had a few years of ethnographic work behind me, spent listening to and observing people who were strangers to my personal history and experience. Describing their cultures and histories, my hosts had all recounted intensely human stories. The 'archeological' and almost psychoanalytical exploration of the narrative symbolics of their identity awakened the idea of the narrative 'excavation' of my own genealogy. Since the early years of my childhood, in the 1950s, I had heard about Dar-Refayil, the multi-family house in which my maternal grandfather's family had lived in Sétif, eastern Algeria. It was frequently evoked by aunts and uncles who had left it to seek their fortunes in the city, Algiers, where I was born. Their descriptions of this house were enigmatic and tantalizing because I had rarely visited it, the war of independence having made travel in the region very dangerous. Family culture was then in the process of transforming Dar-Refayil into the hearth of its origins. Later, after most of my relatives had left Algeria, leaving behind my grandfather, who died in 1960 and was buried in the Sétif cemetery, the myth of Dar-Refayil continued to feed family memory, now in the framework of the experience of deracination. The house was gradually withdrawing from tangible reality and beginning to take root in genealogical memory. As its story came to include, beyond the adventures of the Senoussi family, those of the Jews of Sétif and of the plural society of twentieth-century Algeria – its peoples and cultures, their religions and their relationships, their joys and sorrows – it was becoming the scene of the family epic and the heart of History.

When I undertook the ethnographic excavation of Dar-Refayil's memories, my goal was not simply to collect information about the past of a family and a domestic community, but to explore the semantics of

1

goal *

memory as it was articulated by an uprooted and dispersed group. I planned to investigate the relation of an ethnic immigrant minority to its

thesis * past. In this context, memory becomes the construction of a social and cultural identity whose symbolic terminology tends to challenge the experience of the current reality. The past becomes a strategy for legitimating the present. The house, as it is remembered and described in great material detail, represents a symbolic entrenchment into a human and geographical environment that has vanished. Memory unfolds as a symbolic denial of migration, separation, and cultural strangeness in French society. Dar-Refayil is constructed as an itinerant household, challenging deracination and all the historical upheavals of the second half of the twentieth century.

The house revealed itself, then, as a fascinating repository of culture and meaning. I visited it in my relatives' memories, having missed knowing it physically. Yet this enterprise placed me in an uncomfortable position vis-à-vis the academic discipline in which it had been developed. My previous ethnographic work had been with Jewish groups which shared only part of my personal history; this time I was going to be conducting the ethnography of my own people. As has so often happened in the history of anthropology, my research became a personal quest. Yet was it really different from the ethnographic peregrinations dramatized in *Tristes Tropiques*? In a way, I was going to explore an exotic continent: my Maghrebian tradition and history had become increasingly foreign to me as I had become acculturated into French society and its academic system. The ethnographic survey emphasized my estrangement. My cousins, uncles, and great-aunts, most of whom had not had similar opportunities in French universities, treated me with a mixture of suspicion and admiration. My investigation of our common history at first surprised them: why did I find it worthy of academic interest? They perceived my initiative as a kind of 'astronomy,' observing my genealogy through a telescope as one would a celestial constellation (Lévi-Strauss 1963). Later my project took on a new and ambiguous dimension, evolving as a putting down of new roots alongside my people, subtly intermeshed with the ethnographic distancing. At that point the boundaries between subject and object were blurred by the ambivalence of my position as an observer. I had to question *my* people, in terms of my discipline's methodological conventions. Overall, my research developed as a shuttling between my hosts' and my original culture and the French university culture within which my quest of it arose – between two cultural worlds, that of the colonized and that of the colonizer. This book is the product of this historical and cultural puzzle. Writing it has been an experience of symbolic 'border crossing' (see Behar 1993), but here natives' narratives are not the only ones crossing.

Some of the interviews on which this account is based were collected in the spring of 1979, during three weeks spent in Marseilles, where most of Dar-Refayil's former Jewish residents had settled in 1962. Over the following two years I collected additional narratives during frequent visits to Marseilles for family celebrations. My fieldwork unfolded through both participant observation and interviewing, for reminiscence proved to be part and parcel of many a gathering. I conducted conversations on several fronts. Family reunions around festive tables were obvious mnemonic stimuli, and here my intervention went relatively unnoticed; the Dar-Refayil epic regularly and spontaneously accompanied ritual gatherings. I also interviewed several members of the former household individually. This procedure revealed the diversified production of collective memory by re-creating individual viewpoints on the communal story. Although individual recollections are incorporated into the collective story, their diversity provided the group's epic with the singular dimension of personal experience and pointed to my hosts' conception of the self as rooted in communal identity. I then directed my interrogations towards smaller groups of former residents, women in particular, who frequently assembled in the kitchen for the ritual preparation of festive meals. One of our encounters with memory occurred in a local *hammam*, the public bath. Joining two of my aunts in one of their moments of relaxation between two festive reunions, I was able to record descriptions of similar preritual ablutions as they were practised in Sétif in the past.[1]

Months after these first fieldwork trips, I interviewed other relatives and friends of the household living in the Paris metropolitan area and in southern France. Around the same period, an ethnographic trip to Constantine in May 1979 gave me the opportunity to visit Dar-Refayil for the first time since the departure of most of its Jewish residents. I undertook the long taxi trip to Sétif from Constantine for just a few hours' visit. When I reached the house, I entered the courtyard where some women were occupied with various domestic chores. One of them came towards me and asked whom I wanted to speak to. I chose at random one of the names which had most often come up in the memories of my Jewish informants, and Zakiya was summoned. She was still living in the room where her Jewish former neighbours had known her twenty years earlier. A group of women gathered in the courtyard around her as she came up to me and asked who I was. 'I am Moushi Senoussi's granddaughter', I answered, and general excitement followed. Zakiya kissed me and launched a series of vibrant ululations. The house's former 'concierge', Khadidja, who by this time was very old, kissed my arms whilst reciting Koranic blessings. The merry company began to ask me what had happened to all their former neighbours, now living in France. They wanted a vast range of details about each person's life, habits, and personality. The women then invited me on a guided tour of the house, associating every corner with experiences shared with their former neighbours.

I took my leave of this lively company carrying two 'souvenirs of Dar-Refayil': a traditional embroidered *gandoura* (house robe) and a home-made loaf. Through these gifts my hosts were reestablishing contact with their former neighbours. They were presented as symbols of the domestic world – memories turned into fetishes. The house then seemed a relic, an artefact memory. Although spontaneous, my visit had awakened a dormant process in this Muslim part of the former domestic community. The guided tour was the material reproduction of the symbolic one that my Jewish informants had, through their memories, given me in France – a journey into the past, into a timeless history. My Setifian hosts made me an integral part of a process in the making, one that my ethnographic initiative did not create but awakened. They sought, through that enterprise, to establish contact with their past – a past represented in human form by their former neighbours who had reappeared in their lives like a surrealistic vision with my impromptu visit.

A few weeks after my return to France, I was once again immersed in domestic memories when I received a letter from one of Moushi's former neighbours in Dar-Refayil. Bou-Slimo had moved to an apartment elsewhere in town, but his wife and daughters often visited the house and the friends they still had there. They had been told about my surprising visit, and the letter invited me to return to Sétif for a longer stay:

This will surprise you, but it's Bou-Slimo who is writing to you. I don't know whether you remember us. My wife Sa'adiya remembers you very well, Madeleine, Yvette, Claire, Aimée, Claude, Benjamin, Gilda, and what good neighbours you were. When Mademoiselle Joëlle came, we didn't see her. It is a great pity because we no longer live on the Rue Valée; we now live in Cité Lévy. Only Zakiya, Khlifa's wife, and Latifa and her husband, Kassem, are left in the old house. Farida has also moved, and she sends you her greetings. Zakiya was the one who gave us your address. How are the Akouns, Irène, Denise, Michel, Robert, and Little Mouna? Send them our greetings and give us their address. How is Aimée doing? She's about the same age as my eldest daughter, who teaches French. How are Yvette's children? I believe the eldest is called Jeannette. If Joëlle wanted to come, we would be delighted if she would stay with us. Gilda would often come down and sit up with us, and she would fall asleep sitting on her stool. We had a good time together. I hope you will write back. Together with the whole family, I send you greetings. Give our love to all our old neighbours, old and young.   *Bou-Slimo.*

This letter turned my ethnographic study itself into a system of communication between former Jewish and Muslim neighbours, past and present, France and Algeria, and the two historical parties to colonization. It was sent to my Paris home but was clearly addressed to all the former neighbours; the use of the plural made that clear. My participation in this memory process, suggested and undertaken by my informants themselves, made memory a reversed history: I had been made the bearer of Dar-Refayil's memory. Bou-Slimo had had the letter written by his daughter, the French teacher, in the most elegant and formal language, providing evidence that postcolonial Sétif had not erased French culture as a sign of social advancement.

I accepted the invitation and went back to Sétif the following year, in 1980, to explore the other side of Dar-Refayil's memories. During a month-long stay I saw the Muslim former neighbours of the Senoussi family, some of whom still lived in Dar-Refayil, almost every day. Frequent trips into town allowed me to interview some shopkeepers and other families who were not part of the household itself. During one of my outings in a nearby shopping centre, I visited a bookseller and discreetly enquired about the history of Sétif. Would he have books on the town's history and on its former Jews? He said that he did not know of any such book but suggested that I visit Dar-Refayil and ask the people there. The house was still characterized as a symbolic repository of the Jewish presence in town some two decades after most Jews had left.

Each stage of my enquiry represents a different 'ethnographic encounter' (Crapanzano 1980). The diversity of my contacts, formed in the day-to-day fortunes of fieldwork, ended up being a methodological device that reproduced the cultural, religious, and ethnic plurality of Dar-Refayil's past. My involvement became an integral part of the tale I was asking others to tell me. I was never a mere observer, an outsider to the tale I was excavating. Once again I experienced the ambiguity of the dual position of the outsider engulfed by her object, the position of the native exploring her own ritual from a distance (Altorki and Fawzi-El-Solh 1988).

The reflexive nature of my ethnographic experience was to take on a particular tone when I announced its ultimate goal, writing a book. I came to feel trapped by the consequences of this intervention. From then on I was constantly being questioned about 'the book', its contents, when I would finish writing it, and even who would be acknowledged.[2] This led to a shift in the discourse of my informants, who instead of talking about the *house* now talked about the *book*. At least for a time, the house became a book. I would be told what its narrative and stylistic structure should be, how it should begin and end. This development gave a new and decisive meaning to my project. I was becoming the scribe of an essentially oral tradition, and in so doing I was enhancing my prestige within the family. My manifest indulgence made it possible for my interviewees to manipulate my ethnography to their own ends. Ethnography became *dictation* and the ethnographer the diligent student trying to avoid spelling mistakes.[3] Was my ethnographic enterprise, which had started as the exploration of a non-literate culture, in the process of modifying its object? Was it signalling the end of a culture – serving as its requiem? After all, what does one do with a vanishing culture but hasten to preserve its remains? The shift that my interrogation had generated from orality to the written word raised fundamental epistemological questions. Yet, paradoxically, writing this hitherto oral culture turned into a 'lettering' process. I came to see my project as the granting of a diploma to 'untutored memories' (Rubinstein 1979), to a tradition which academic recognition had only partly legitimated.[4] My informants became the heroes of what began to be perceived as a legend; their vanished world was about to be immortalized. I was transforming their banal story of ordinary people into an exemplary and heroic tale through the magic of the written word. Their memories turned into archives, and their past experiences were given the literary form revered and considered sacred in the Jewish tradition. The writing of this memory of struggling to survive the dangers of History ultimately resulted in its sacralization and perpetuation. I had been placed in a position unusual in ethnography. The literary aim of my project did not endow me with the symbolic authority of the author (Clifford and Marcus 1986:17; Herzfeld 1987:40); rather, my object had infiltrated its investigation. What is presented here is not ethnography as objectification (Bourdieu 1977) but ethnography as the subjectification of the object. As formerly colonized people subjugated by the dominant literate word of the colonial power, my informants had never been given a chance to tell their story. My turning on the tape recorder to write an academic book was perceived as a chance to challenge official colonial history. As a certified and educated scribe, I view my written ethnography as participation in this process of cultural decolonization.

The idea of writing this book exposed me to the double face of ethnography as a literary project (Marcus and Fischer 1986, Marcus and Cushman 1982, Geertz 1988, Jamin 1985). How was I to resolve this dilemma? How could I convey the specific tone of the discourse of an uprooted memory, the stylistic, grammatical, and syntactical awkwardness in the language used by the narrators, the emotions which accompanied the telling of past tragedies? How could I expose the ambiguity of my own relation to this singular anthropological object in whose history I was personally involved? What devices were available for revealing the censorship, the obliteration, and the embellishment which memory uses to translate the past? At the core of these questions lies the issue of the identity and Otherness of the author (Benveniste 1989:16). Who is the Other in this book? Should one look for it in the voices I intend to broadcast or in my own voice, infiltrating my informants' narratives? Is the Otherness in my investigation, so often incongruent with academic discourse, or is it in the inevitable distance between what follows and the native discourse it attempts to convey? These pages reveal a situation of multifaceted reflexivity in which the voices of the Other have been incorporated into my own (Ruby 1982, Fabian 1983, Herzfeld 1987). The ethnographic writing I present here is indeed pregnant with this reflexive process; my voice and those of my informants are constantly exchanging status and violating the boundaries imposed by academic literary convention, producing what Bakhtin described as a plurilinguistic poetics (1978). Writing memory became the axiom of my experiencing bivocality (Fischer 1986), the overlapping of voices, of subject and object. I made myself my informants' ghost writer, my ethnography their collective autobiography. When, as here, the 'natives' manipulate the ethnographer's work by dictating their culture, ethnography becomes a *meta-interpretation* of culture. The eventual ethnographic text is made up of several layers of cultural discourse, including that of the natives on their own culture.

In his *New Critical Essays*, Roland Barthes declared that Proust's *La Recherche du temps perdu* is a story of writing (1980:55). In this twentieth-century literary monument, translated into English as *Remembrance of Things Past*, the narrative structure unfolds as successive sequences of a rite of initiation in which the narrator first discovers his drive to sense the world and to write it, then experiences impotence as a writer, and finally recovers the initial drive when he reconciles the world of the senses with that of the Book – the Book becomes the world, the world the Book. This reconciliation is a process of memory: literature is a journey through time, and *La Recherche du temps perdu* should have been translated *In Search of Time Lost*. Proust's search presented memory, perhaps for the first time in literature, as a full-fledged literary process. To remember is to recover the original drive for writing. Moreover, in Proust's novel, this search for time lost unfolds as a geographical journey in space between the provincial Combray, a world of learning senses, and Paris, a world of writing them.

The spatial structure of *La Recherche* is articulated, according to Barthes, as a tension between the Combray of the past, of childhood and tradition, and the Paris of literature, maturity, modernity, and social advancement. This structure represents the biographical and geographical dilemma of writing, a tension between past and present which the book aims to resolve as its writing becomes memory resolution. As such, the search for time lost is also a search for space lost, a process that Bakhtin was later to conceptualize in his notion of the 'chronotope' (1978).

As an ethnographer of Dar-Refayil's memories, I have experienced Proustian wanderings into the written rite of initiation, and the process is still going on today. After the French publication of the book in 1992 (Bahloul 1992b), I received several calls from my informants expressing their excitement on reading the volume. They also told me with amusement that they had started to call each other by the fictitious names I had given them in the book. Thus, as Proust's village of Illiers was rebaptized Combray after the publication of *La Recherche*, my ethnographic fiction entered my informants' reality and fiction and reality merged in the writing project. Collective memory claimed to become a historical discourse while being written from an outsider's viewpoint. The distinction between memory and history appeared, then, to be, as Halbwachs suggested (1980), one of symbolic legitimation.

As have other anthropologists who have used the technique of biographical interviewing, I have often wondered as I was listening to my informants' accounts whether the ethnographic situation was not likely to amplify the epic nature of the tale I was being told. Doubtless the presence of the tape recorder and the reference to the book project would have contributed to this process. My informants were trying to bring their answers as close as possible to the literary project that they knew was my goal. Their discourse seemed ready to be heard, recorded, and written, as if memory had already done its rhetorical work before I began to ask.[5] Another bias in my treatment of my informants' narratives is its focus on a particular subgroup. The book focuses on the biography of a particular family, the Senoussis, as if that of the other residents were defined by it. This family appears as a social and cultural kernel, the parent of the narrative. Its history is presented as a narrative seed. This is partially the result of my personal involvement in the ethnographic collection: the Senoussis comprise the maternal side of my genealogy, and my enquiry started with their narratives. At the same time, they are the ones who suggested and facilitated contacts with other former neighbours and served as source-brokers for my fieldwork.

Despite these methodological manipulations, my ethnographic rendition aims to focus on the power of the collected word over ethnographic discourse. Rather than complacently deciphering the literal aspect of my ethnographic text (Crapanzano 1980, Rabinow 1977), my goal is to retain the textuality of the collected document and to be 'faithful to the text' (Lévi-Strauss 1987b:117). In the following pages voices should resonate between the lines. I found the structure of my ethnographic writing in the narrative devices used by my informants. This gives me the opportunity to address the central issue in this study: the articulation of identity in narrative memory.

The collective memory presented here is a specific type of memorial elaboration mainly supported by narrative. It is also an *oral* narrative memory. The analysis thus straddles several human scientific approaches – the theory of narrative, life-history ethnography, and oral history. My ethnographic account crosses the strict boundaries of these diverse methodologies to produce what I would call a reflexive ethnographic text. The question of collective identity is obviously at the core of this problematic, and it assumes a special character when viewed through the prism of the theory of narrative. Although focused on the past of a group of families, this account deals mostly with their identity in the present: the way they have chosen to express it underlines the power of oral narrative in the construction of ethnic identity (Boyarin 1991, Fischer 1986). It is also founded on a specific conception of time, which is made *identity time* in uprooted memory: in a sense, remembered time is a substitute for geography in migrants' cosmology. Narrative memory negotiates time and space to locate the migrant group – to create a new symbolic place for it in history. Another structural aspect of the relation between narrative memory and ethnic identity is to be found in its performative construction: the oral narration of Dar-Refayil's story suggests the presence of an audience and a transmission system with specific social procedures. Ritual and family gatherings are the key moments for the emergence of narrative recollections. The procedure points to the identity function of both narrative memory and the social settings in which it emerges (ritual and the family).

Narrative memory involves two levels of signification: that of historical discourse and consciousness, and that of the reconstruction of factual historical data. The specificity of narrative is that it combines these two levels, and I have chosen to do the same. What follows is a typical ethnohistorical account that does not simplistically transform and manipulate the past but essentially reappropriates global history phenomenologically

(Sahlins 1981): history is here particularized through the re-enactment of past *experiences*.

The voices heard here have rushed into my tape recorder with the particular rhythm and sound of the place that inspires and structures them. I have tried to write this book accordingly, following the physical, visual, and spatial tone of my hosts' words and incorporating the sounds and images of the lost domestic space. Along these material lines, the household takes shape as a social and cultural entity. Human beings and their lives gradually emerge from the descriptions of physical space. This is particularly clear in the story of the group's founding. The epic begins with the Senoussis' arrival in Dar-Refayil, and this arrival is presented as the logical result of the settlement there of members of the same family stock as far back as the beginning of the century. The settling in the house is the founding motif of the genealogical tale. The house is like a family, and in its history the family appears as solid as a built structure. As we go through the house, memories not only describe physical space but also tell a social history. Domestic space serves as a metaphor for the human entity that inhabits it. Domestic space is the space of memory.

As these recollections were narrated to me, they focused upon three narrative structures: the spatial, the social, and the temporal. The structure of the book follows this narrative order. The first chapter explores the events selected as the commencement of the domestic epic. The second chapter aims to convey the memories' sense of space and discusses the significant way in which places 'speak' about the past and people re-enact their past by rebuilding past places. The third chapter is concerned with the social contents of the epic. Here memories humanize the domestic space with people's movements, interactions, and fates. They sketch the image of the house along social lines, and built structure is physically and socially occupied. The fourth chapter deciphers the temporal structure of the memorial narratives; it discusses the meaning of dates and of the pacing of domestic time as it is narrated and indicates how a household's story becomes History. Finally, the last chapter proposes an analysis of the multidimensional functioning of the poetics of remembrance.

1

Foundations

During the colonial era, local Jews considered Sétif a boom town with 'fervour', with unique personality (Laloum 1987:154). It became a full-fledged *commune de plein exercice* (a municipally governed community) in 1854 and then the *sous-prefecture* of the Constantine *département* (regional district) in 1858. Located some 130 kilometres west of Constantine and by the early twentieth century a crossroads for regional trade, Sétif experienced a period of great economic and demographic growth after the First World War. In the thirties, it was an urban community of just over thirty thousand residents, growing to 53,000 towards the end of the fifties and to 96,000 just before Algerian independence in 1962 (Camborieux 1978:122; Gouvernement Général de l'Algérie 1922).

Algerian Jews had been granted French citizenship by the Crémieux Decree in 1870. In the following decades they made an effort to become integrated into colonial society, as did other non-French Europeans, Spaniards, Italians, Maltese, Swiss, and Germans, who had settled in this colonized country. After the 1870 Franco-Prussian War these immigrants were joined by flocks of settlers from Alsace-Lorraine who had refused to become German (Camborieux 1978:69). Towards the end of the nineteenth century, the Jewish population of Sétif consisted of about 180 families, or 1,600 people (Alliance Israélite Universelle, Algérie, I.C.1),[1] around 15 per cent of the local population. It had two synagogues and a substantial communal infrastructure. Its leaders were recruited from among local grain traders, physicians, and attorneys. Fund-raising campaigns had been organized by Setifian Jews in the early 1880s to assist the Russian Jews who were then suffering pogroms (Alliance Israélite Universelle, Algérie, IV.B.25). Jewish immigration in Sétif reached a peak between the end of the nineteenth century and the end of the First World

War, although there were anti-Jewish incidents in 1920 (Alliance Israélite Universelle, Algérie, I.C.1). Among the new settlers were Jews from Morocco, from Tétouan in particular (Leibovici 1984; my ethnographic sources). In addition, Jews from nearby rural communities had moved in since the beginning of the century to take advantage of the town's economic prosperity. At the turn of the century, more than 10 per cent of the local population was Jewish, and this rose to 13 per cent after the First World War (*Encyclopedia Judaica* 1971: *s.v.* 'Algeria').[2]

Yet the economic position of this Jewish community was never very strong (Alliance Israélite Universelle, Algérie, IV.B.25). The Jewish population of Sétif declined sharply between the two world wars, falling from 3,015 in 1921 to under 2,000 in the fifties, while the rest of the population tripled. Rabbi Eisenbeth noted in 1930 that over 65 percent of the Setifian Jewish population then in the workforce were manual labourers or craftsmen.[3] No fewer than 90 were cobblers and 39 seamstresses – this in a community of about 2,000. However, there were at the same time 34 Jewish accountants: some Jews had succeeded in overcoming colonial barriers and in gaining access to professional education and careers which formerly only a few Jews had practised. Many of the 157 Jewish merchants were involved in trading foodstuffs then designated 'colonial produce' (mainly cereals) and 'indigenous textiles' (Eisenbeth 1931). The three Jewish farmers of Sétif were respected for their position within colonial society and for the leadership functions they performed within the Jewish community alongside a few professionals and civil servants. The socioeconomic make-up of the Setifian Jewish community in the 1930s reveals its intermediate status between native Muslims and European Christians while most of its members were actually clinging to the lowest rungs of the social ladder. Though gradually introduced to occupations traditionally reserved for 'Europeans', local Jews retained a respected status in indigenous society through their economic, linguistic, and cultural exchanges with the Muslim community.

These characteristics were reflected in their geographical distribution. A number of them resided near the commercial area, around the downtown market, and lived next to Muslim families. In their descriptions of the town, Dar-Refayil veterans emphasize its integrated structure. Sétif is remembered as a town with no significant *geographical* distinction along religious and ethnic lines. There was no Jewish or Muslim quarter; Jews were scattered throughout the town in accordance with their social status. Ethnic diversity was most noticeable in certain neighbourhoods – the Rue

Valée, the Rue d'Aumale, and the Rue d'Isly along the Rue du Général Sarrail and around the covered market (figure 1.1) where Jewish and Muslim merchants pre-dominated.

The buildings in this neighbourhood were of various architectural styles. The two prevailing ones pointed up the plural nature of this small colonial town. The first consisted of three- to four-storey apartment buildings with wrought iron balconies and represented a European-type lifestyle. The second type was a low two-storey building consisting of an inner courtyard around which were several rooms that communicated with one another. In this latter type of building, a single gate gave access to the whole of the house. The inner rooms opened onto the courtyard or the balconied gallery; apartments consisting of several adjacent rooms had doors into the rooms next door. Despite the conspicuously large number of doors (suggesting a highly differentiated household), these houses' interiors were quite permeable: doors were always left open or reduced to a curtain or a reed screen. Buildings of this style were mainly inhabited by native Algerian families, Jewish or Muslim. Intimacy was

Figure 1.1 Sétif in the 1940s; the house is shown by the initials D. R.

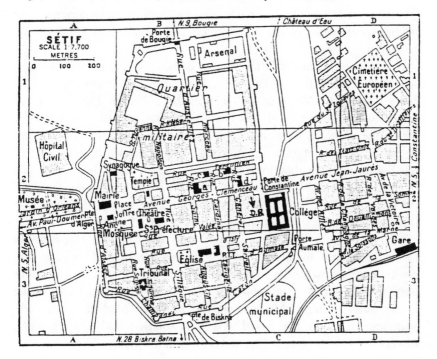

their architectural trope, suggesting that inhabitants were related or bound by occupational, religious, or social ties.[4] In Sétif these houses tended to be occupied by multiethnic family groups, for the most part Jewish and Muslim. Jewish families only rarely shared their domestic space with Christian ones, and it was even rarer for Christian and Muslim families to live side by side.

Dar-Refayil stood at the beginning of the Rue Valée in the midst of a neighbourhood in which this second architectural type structured both the physical and the social landscape. One gained access to the house through a gate which opened onto a cobbled, rectangular, open-air inner courtyard (figure 1.2). On the ground floor there were about thirteen rooms, each of roughly ten square metres along three walls of the courtyard. The first floor had a similar layout; only the apartment along the front had windows facing onto the street. The owners of the building lived here, thus physically separated from the rest of the residents, who were all tenants. This distinction between tenants and owners was materially marked not only by the direction in which the windows opened but also by an individual front door located at the top of a staircase that was reserved for them. By contrast, tenants occupied rooms always open to all and laid out along a communal gallery. Dar-Refayil's memories emphasize this social and architectural design, pointing to the predominance of socioeconomic over religious differences in the organization and structure of the domestic community.

Additional evidence of this is provided by the house's namesake, a Jew called Refayil who had owned it since the beginning of the century and who had died well before the 1930s. In 1954 the house was sold to another local Jew but kept its tenants and the name by which the domestic community had been known in town for decades. In Sétif residents of this sort of building were known by the name of the house in which they lived. Individual identity was determined less by surnames than by the name of one's dwelling. One would speak of Rachel of Dar-Zmemra (the Zemmours' house), David of Dar-Warda (the house of roses), or of René, a son of Dar-Braydjiyin (the house of the Bordjians). Despite migration and deracination, Dar-Refayil's former residents maintain this naming system for identifying and positioning themselves in history. Now settled in France and in other parts of Algeria, they are still 'the children of Dar-Refayil', as if the house were a parent. Much as in the northern Mediterranean rural societies based on the *oustal* system (Lamaison and Claverie 1982, Rogers 1991) and certain Maghrebian societies (Bedoucha 1980, 1987;

Geertz 1979), social identity in colonial Algeria was established mainly by residence.[5]

It is in this enclosed and differentiated world that Moushi Senoussi and his family found themselves in 1937, after the trauma of his wife's death.

Figure 1.2 Plan of the house

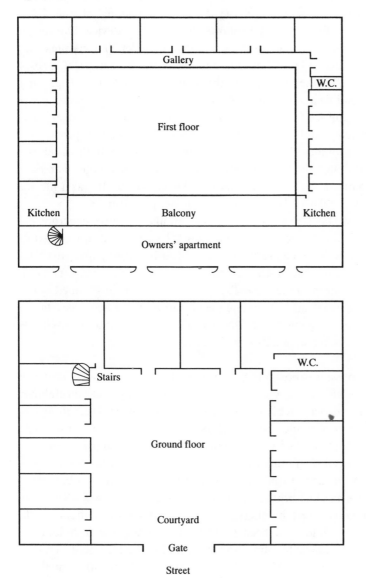

Death as beginning
Death appears as a founding event in a great number of myths of origin. The origin of the group and of its culture is narratively placed after a death as if death generated life – as if it were symbolically constructed as a creative act. At the same time, this symbolic process is likely to name a group's founding ancestor, often an eponymous one. In the Jewish tradition, an important section of the daily ritual reading of the Torah (Pentateuch) in the synagogue follows this narrative device. During the religious festival of Simhat Torah,[6] the faithful complete the reading of the Pentateuch's fifth book (Deuteronomy) with the narration of Moses' death. Then, after they have rolled the manuscript back to its beginning, they begin reading again with the creation of the universe. In a number of Jewish communities this ritual reading is accompanied by dancing and rejoicing which unambiguously celebrate the biblical values of procreation and fertility (Goldberg 1987:107). The mythology relating to these celebrations and the unfolding of the ritual include a key symbolic pattern in Jewish religious thought, the continuity of life and death. It is as if life and death were interrelated elements of a narrative opposition.

The story of Dar-Refayil is governed by a similar narrative structure. For the Senoussi family, memory begins in 1937 with the death of Sarah, Moushi's first wife, and ends in 1960 with Moushi's death, after which the last Senoussis and other Jewish residents left the house and then left Algeria to begin a new life in France. Dar-Refayil's memoirs are thus framed by two deaths. These two deaths punctuate the narration of the Senoussis' family autobiography. They emphasize the fact that the household saw itself as a genealogical world and that its story is above all a family epic.

Moushi Senoussi was born in 1898 in Bordj-Bou-Arreridj, a rural market town some 70 kilometres west of Sétif. He was the sixth of eleven children. His parents owned a butcher shop which was probably not large enough to support so large a family. After the First World War, the economic recession and the high level of unemployment in the small semirural towns of this region forced the family to sell the business and scatter. As a second son, Moushi managed to salvage enough money to set up as a butcher in Sétif, whereas his elder brother left to seek his fortune in Algiers. Several of Moushi's relatives were butchers as well, an occupation with which the extended family had long been familiar. They knew the techniques of cattle breeding and meat cutting, and above all they had the necessary contacts with the regional Arab breeders who supplied them with animals for slaughter. Moushi was known in Sétif as El-Braydji (the man from Bordj or, alternatively, from the countryside). The pun identified him both geographically as a sort of outsider, and socioculturally as the opposite of an urbanite, which was becoming a sign of class distinction in the thriving Sétif of the 1920s. This system of identification also and no less significantly addressed the depth of Moushi's integration into the rural Arab-Muslim society: it was the Jews of rural origin who maintained close links with the regional Arabs, spoke perfect Arabic (which was their mother tongue), and had a lifestyle and traditions closely related to those of their Muslim neighbours.

Moushi quickly made a place for himself in Sétif's Jewish community, which at the time consisted mainly of small shopkeepers and craftsmen. In 1922, at the age of twenty-four, he married Sarah, the third child and second daughter of David the hairdresser (*el-haffef*). Sarah was twenty-one when she married and had three brothers and eight sisters. According to Sarah's children, in particular her eldest daughter, David's family was quite 'progressive'[7] for its time. David had managed to provide all his children, including his daughters, with a decent secular education. One of Sarah's brothers became a schoolteacher, and most of her sisters graduated from elementary school. The so-called *certificat d'études* (elementary school degree) was viewed as no mean achievement for women of that generation in a highly patriarchal society. Later on, Sarah encouraged her own children to acquire a high level of education and to pursue careers in education. Although she rarely spoke Arabic to them, they remember her flattering them by calling them *oulad rumiya* (the children of a Christian mother), implying that they were as spoiled, pampered, and well educated as the children of the most 'progressive' European families. Evidently, by avoiding Arabic in her daily communication with her children and by pressing them to succeed in the (French) classroom, Sarah was paving the way for them to become perfect Frenchmen and Frenchwomen. This policy of social advancement was implemented in most Jewish communities of the Mediterranean and the French colonies elsewhere through the integration of children, regardless of gender, into the French education system or the Alliance Israélite Universelle network. Sarah's story emphasizes that, contrary to the stereotype of North African Jewish women (Bensimon-Donath 1962), mothers were not passive in this regard, even in the 1930s.

Sarah went through seven pregnancies, two of which ended in miscarriage. She therefore raised five children, two girls and three boys. Madeleine, the eldest, was born in 1923, Marcel in 1925, Edouard (known as Eddie) in 1928, Yvette in 1930, and Charles (known as Charlie) in 1935

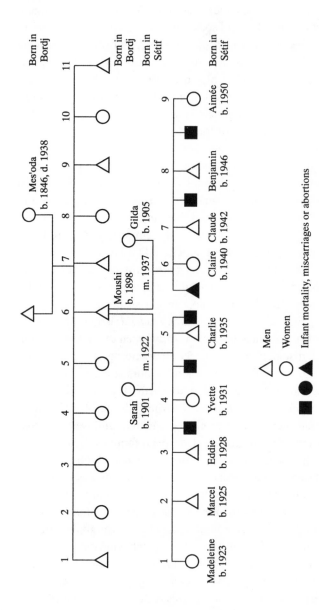

Figure 1.3 The Senoussis (genealogy)

(figure 1.3). Between her marriage in 1922 and her death in 1937, Sarah became pregnant about every eighteen months. During these fifteen years, it was she who managed her husband's business in addition to fulfilling her responsibilities as a mother of five. The women of her generation had no alternative but to endure one of two forms of physical suffering: repeated pregnancies, or death as a result of a botched abortion. Birth control was unknown in this highly family-oriented Jewish society. The rabbis, who exerted considerable influence on the private life of local Jews, either knew nothing about birth control or discouraged its use. Moreover, men and women of that time knew scarcely anything about family planning. In the 1930s, anything related to family health was viewed as pertaining to *mektub* (destiny or divine governance), which folk beliefs sought to conjure through expedient therapeutics. Some women used parsley concoctions which were said to provoke abortion when injected in the vaginal cavity. Others used hot sitz-baths. Others entrusted themselves to the care of a neighbour who would attempt to expel the foetus with a knitting needle. Sarah probably resorted to this last technique when she found herself pregnant for the eighth time. Reluctant to carry this pregnancy to term because of her heavy domestic schedule, she tried to abort or 'miscarry', as it was called then. She was 'doctored'[8] by a neighbour and subsequently died of a severe infection. Through her story, Sarah's children describe the tragic dilemma of the women of this small traditional town. Her death resounds in their memory like a suffering woman's screams. Sarah's body as a female world becomes a narrative trope in the construction of Dar-Refayil's story. It was Sarah's body that gave birth to the domestic community; it was her body that gave birth to narrative memory, and every line of this memory is bodily.[9]

The year 1937 was particularly harsh for the daughters of David the hairdresser: two weeks before Sarah's death, two of her younger sisters, Sultana and Rose, then aged seventeen and fourteen, had died of typhoid. As a family friend, Rolande G., remembered it when I interviewed her in the summer of 1989, this was a tragedy for the entire Jewish community of Sétif. The community and the Senoussi family in particular interpreted it as the failure of motherhood and saw it as a challenge to the institution of the family itself. Sarah's death dramatically called into question the community's familism by showing that the woman's body suffered from these values as well as reproducing them. Years later, it is the women who remember this major event most vividly. In this narrative construction, they indicate how they struggled to recover the control over their own bodies of which the community had dispossessed them by treating a woman's body as a collective property in the service of the community's social reproduction (Martin 1987:104). Through Sarah's tragedy they interpreted backstreet abortion as both part of women's oppression and a rebellion against the community's dictates.[10] Jewish women in prewar Sétif were developing a new conception of social reproduction not restricted to its biological and demographic dimensions. They were attempting to point out that the community's social reproduction could be better secured through social advancement than through high fertility rates. This view was incompatible with their traditional role as mothers.[11]

Her mother's death had a lasting impact on Madeleine, who was fourteen when it took place. Her reminiscence of it is the most poignant of all. Her younger brothers and sister barely remember the event; their ages at the time ranged between two and twelve. My questions stimulated only a vague memory of their mother, and they seemed to have reconstructed her story through relatives' reports. They remembered more clearly the wanderings that followed their mother's death. The family celebrated, together with the tragedy's first month memorial, the bar mitzvah of Marcel, who retained a fragmented memory of the whole event. The pastries served at the party had been carefully prepared by Sarah in her last months. For Marcel, this bar mitzvah was funereal. By contrast Madeleine can reconstruct most of the event's details half a century later. She tells the story as an orphan reenacting the emotions of the past, as if they had been frozen at the time of her mother's death – as if her words repeatedly were reburying her mother. Her narrative is a timeless funeral. 'This was the darkest part of my life', she said time and again. Her mother's death, turned into a sort of mythical narrative of the generic death of the generic mother, was the most painful possible introduction to womanhood. She had already become in part the woman that her mother had brought her up to be: Sarah had sewed the same dresses for her daughter as for herself and encouraged Madeleine in her school work with great care and concern. Sarah knew that if her daughter was to avoid the troubles that the women of her generation had experienced, she would have to obtain the highest school degrees. 'She was my big sister and my friend rather than my mother', said Madeleine forty years later. In the 1930s, the adolescent was learning from her mother how to rebel against the prevailing view of the female condition, of which the mother was to be a victim.

Madeleine lost an ally when her mother died. The community, through the intervention of the rabbi and some relatives, regained control over the family by encouraging Moushi to remarry as soon as possible. Sarah's death had generated an imbalance that needed to be corrected. And while a distraught Moushi, overwhelmed by grief, was losing control over his business and family responsibilities, the children were left on their own, 'abandoned', the women say. As the eldest daughter, Madeleine looked after her younger brothers and sister and took over her dead mother's tasks. After school, she cleaned the house, prepared the meals, and bathed the youngest, Charlie, who was not yet two years old. When some cousins offered to take over these tasks, they also took advantage of the children's naïvety and emptied the house of all the valuables, jewels, and embroidered linens that Sarah had carefully kept for her children. After this the children were entrusted to a distant aunt who did not really want them. In the end, having found no support among their maternal relatives, they went to live with Moushi's aged mother, Mes'oda. Following the rabbi's advice, she suggested that Moushi remarry. 'This household needs a mother!' said the women. Motherhood had to be salvaged.

The deceased's sisters were the first marriageable women to be put forward. Traditionally, the sororate was often chosen by the community as a convenient recourse for families broken by a wife's death.[12] However, the prospective candidates rejected the idea; Jewish tradition was not going to open the way to the emancipation they yearned for. Mes'oda then thought of one of her 'distant cousins',[13] Gilda, who was then thirty-two years old and keeping house for her maternal aunt and adoptive mother.[14] The marriage of Moushi and Gilda, celebrated only a few months after Sarah's death, is described as the salvation of the institution of the family on two fronts. For the Senoussis it generated the return of a mother to their household. For the community it meant the termination of a painful spinsterhood.

Moushi and Gilda went on to have four children: Claire, born in 1940, Claude, born in 1942, Benjamin, born in 1946, and Aimée, born in 1950. Gilda eventually experienced failed motherhood too: she had two miscarriages and lost a baby boy in his first year. By the standards of her society, she was a latecomer to motherhood and had no great talent for child rearing. She was not the supportive mother that Sarah had been to Madeleine, never having acquired the subtleties of maternal care in which Sarah was an expert. She had hardly any education and was not concerned about it. Madeleine willingly helped her run the house, often on her own initiative. Eventually, Madeleine dropped out of school and took a job to supplement the family income neglected by an inconsolable Moushi.

This was the frame of mind in which the new Senoussi household moved to Dar-Refayil at the end of 1937, having left an apartment in what Madeleine characterizes as an opulent high-rise building on the Rue d'Aumale. At the time, a house in which someone had died was believed to be cursed, and the arrival of Moushi and his children in Dar-Refayil is viewed as the family's salvation. However, this move also marked a decline in the family's fortunes. The children's education, which Sarah had promoted, ended with her death.[15] In addition to Madeleine's dropping out of school, Marcel, whom Sarah had envisioned as a future teacher, went to work in the butcher shop with his father. The relative comfort which Sarah had carefully arranged in the Rue d'Aumale apartment was replaced in Dar-Refayil by overcrowding and lack of privacy. In Dar-Refayil the Senoussis had to share their domestic space with Arab families, which too was viewed as a sign of reduced prestige: the Jews of the time, who were in the process of initial Westernization and laborious social advancement, viewed the Arab lifestyle as the epitome of social backwardness. Moushi spoke Arabic with his new, uneducated wife, whereas he had formerly spoken French with Sarah to make it easier for their children to become integrated into French culture and schooling. Thus it is no surprise that Madeleine remembers the move as a gigantic step backward for the entire family. Yet in Dar-Refayil's memories as a whole, Sarah's death and the arrival of the bereaved family in the house are presented as the events leading to the founding of the domestic group. In Dar-Refayil the mother was replaced and the family expanded with the birth of more children, and the Senoussis found a ready-made community of neighbours, some of whom were relatives. Eventually additional family ties were created through marriages within the domestic community.

For most of its former residents now established in France, Dar-Refayil appears as a mother-house, a built structure which, with its inner court-yard described as a womb, embodies the motherhood that had been lost with Sarah's death. In women's narratives, the image of the mother-house is associated with their rejection of motherhood as a public service. The story of Dar-Refayil as a mother-house unfolds as advocacy for private motherhood as opposed to motherhood for the community's sake. For the women, the narrative is a verbal strategy for recovering their bodies. The narrated house is shaped like a female body; it is a physical universe, and the narrated places are embodied places – places inscribed in the body.

A tale of motherhood
Motherhood thus lies at the heart of Dar-Refayil's founding tale and constitutes its narrative structure. What we are dealing with is the story of motherhood wounded and then revived. Yet this tale is not a mere homage to motherhood. To the contrary, it is strewn with contradictions, dis-

cursive ambiguities, and symbolic reversals. It is as if its narrative wanderings traced the wanderings of Sarah's despairing orphans. The family and motherhood are initially celebrated with Sarah's virtues, her care for her children and spouse. In the first part of the narrative, the family appears in its positive aspect with the image of the perfect mother. Then Sarah dies for rejecting the excessive demands of this perfect motherhood, and the discursive pattern is turned around. The *maternal* family – namely Sarah's sisters and brothers – is struck by disaster and abandons the orphans to their fate. The female cousins ransack the deceased woman's household. The failure of motherhood leaves the family in shambles. This second part of the narrative draws upon a negative representation of the family. Eventually, as a last resort, there is a symbolic return to the point of departure: the institution of the family is rescued by the relatives' solidarity backed by rabbinical authority, and a second marriage is engineered resulting in the recovery of motherhood. Behind the scenes of this story is a shift from the valuation of motherhood to the restoration of paternal control. In effect it is Moushi's relatives who encourage him to remarry; it is his relatives whom he finds when he settles his new household in Dar-Refayil, and what the female memories describe there is a highly patriarchal universe.

The Senoussis' fate is a discursive balance between maternal and paternal narrative models. This narrative order is memory's discursive rendition of the contradictions inherent in prewar Setifian society, a familist endogamous community that swallowed up women by imposing motherhood on them as martyrdom. The founding tale of Dar-Refayil is a discursive system in which the family struggles with itself and with the ideology that fosters it in a society that is fighting to survive. The Jewish population was just over 2,000 in the 1930s, and emigration was reducing that number daily. Moreover, the political situation had become more threatening when, in the summer of 1934, a pogrom broke out in Constantine that claimed the lives of twenty-five Jews.[16] In the following months, the Jewish communities of the region's small towns were repeatedly threatened, particularly in Sétif, where the Jews were alarmed in February 1935 by a rebellion directed specifically against the town's military contingent 'Indigenous'[17] gunmen attacked the police station after one of them had been killed by a police officer. The rumor spread that the officer in question was Jewish. Some Jewish shops near the police station were plundered and anti-Jewish slogans were heard during the attack. The attackers also took on the police's financial representative, an Alsatian Jew accused of collaborating with the colonial power. Arab pamphlets reminded the Jews:

'You were once our subjects, do not forget this! We are asking you not to get involved in the current dispute between us and the colonial rulers.'[18]

Ultimately, the Jews were threatened both politically and socially. The community was experiencing a severe economic crisis and unemployment that affected mainly small shopkeepers. During the interwar period, anti-Semitism was widespread and ferocious in the Christian population and made it very difficult for the Jews to become integrated into European society. The family and endogamy were viewed as institutional shields in this critical situation. When these were also in decline, the entire community feared for its life. Through its ambivalent narrative tropes, Dar-Refayil's founding tale expresses this uncertainty of the Jewish condition.

The domestic community: a web of family ties
The presence of the Senoussi lineage in Dar-Refayil dates to its settlement in Sétif in the early twenties. A distant cousin of Moushi's was already living in the house at the time, and all its residents were Jewish. Nonna, Moushi's maternal aunt, who lived there with her children, had indicated to her sister Mes'oda that an apartment adjacent to hers was available in the house for Moushi's family. The domestic community was already framed by Moushi's kin group; it was a genealogical community, and many of its Jewish residents were related (figure 1.4). In addition to Nonna, Ma Sultana, a cousin of Moushi's, lived there with her children. Four other Jewish families eventually resided in Dar-Refayil. The Bakoushes arrived there in 1945 from Tébessa, a small town south-east of Sétif, near the Tunisian border. Along with other Tébessa Jews they had fled the Nazi advance through North Africa after many Tunisian Jews had been rounded up during the war. A woman known as Little Mouna resided in Dar-Refayil with her four children and her husband, who, after they separated, rented an adjacent room in the courtyard. The Dahans were there, too, with their children, and the Karoubys, the house's owners, occupied the front apartment until they sold the house to the Akoun family in 1954. A large part of the domestic community was in fact named Akoun: Anna and Mardochée; Little Mouna; and Ma Sultana and her daughter, both of whom married Akouns. Finally, Raoul the printer owned a shop which opened onto the courtyard (figure 1.5). Later, Muslim families occupied rooms around the courtyard. This spatial distinction between Muslim and Jewish families persisted until the departure of the latter, just before independence. In the Jewish residents' descriptions it represents a symbolic hierarchy which unfolded in a practical form in the local social structure. Jews had only a slightly higher status than Muslims. The rent for

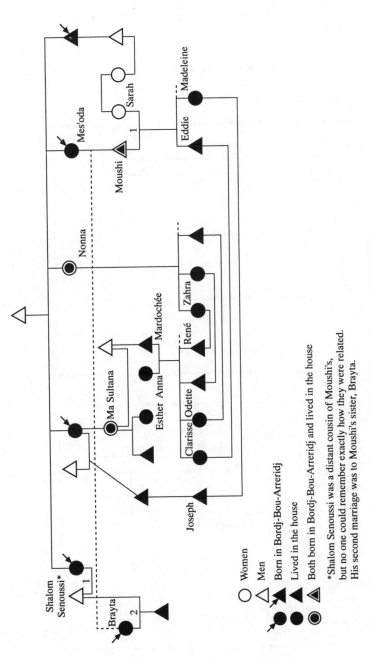

Figure 1.4 The complex web of family ties

Shalom Senoussi*

Brayta

Ma Sultana

Nonna

Mes'oda

Moushi

Sarah

Esther Anna

Mardochée

Zahra

René

Madeleine

Eddie

Clarisse Odette

Joseph

○ Women

◁ Men

◀ Born in Bordj-Bou-Arreridj

◀ Lived in the house

◁ Both born in Bordj-Bou-Arreridj and lived in the house

*Shalom Senoussi was a distant cousin of Moushi's,
but no one could remember exactly how they were related.
His second marriage was to Moushi's sister, Brayta.

ground-floor rooms was not much higher than that for first-floor apartments, but the latter were closer to the owners' apartment, and the
Senoussis, living in an apartment adjacent to the owners', were allowed to
use their balcony for the celebration of bar-mitzvahs and other life-cycle
rituals. In Jewish discourse the spatial distribution of Jewish and Muslim

Figure 1.5 The occupancy of the house

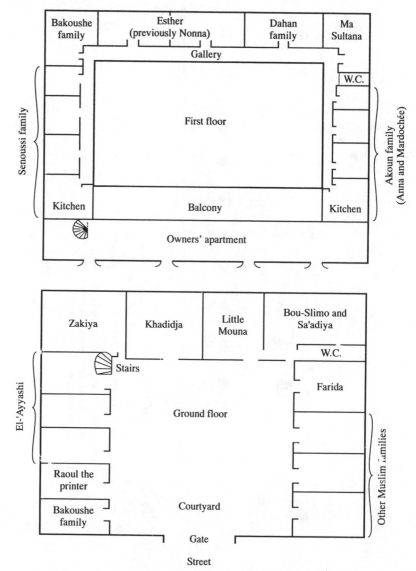

families reflects a socioeconomic and ethnic distinction. For those Jews who were striving to become integrated into the European community in Algeria, the more they could distinguish themselves from the Muslim community, the greater their chances of being accepted amongst the French. Memory emphasizes difference and separation in the description of the dense and self-contained world in which Jews and Muslims grew up side by side. Living in the rooms around the courtyard meant being closer to the Muslims, thus farther away from French culture.

On the Muslim side, Dar-Refayil included eight families who had gradually settled in since the early forties. These included the families of Bou-Slimo and Zakiya, the concierge Khadidja, who took care of the housekeeping and locked the gate at night, Farida and her children, El-'Ayyashi the 'dentist',[19] and three other families. In all, Dar-Refayil included about thirty rooms and some eighteen families, with an average of seventy-five to eighty residents. Memory emphasizes this density through underscored descriptions of overcrowding, as if it were a sort of Tower of Babel,[20] a domestic community whose only common denominators were its genealogical structure and the predominance of kinship ties within it. Family-based values and relationships were paramount in this world of multiple cultures, languages, and religions, where people whose diverse social and historical fortunes remained sharply distinguished even though they encountered each other every day. The family and its moral values were the cement of a society criss-crossed by differences.

2

Telling places: the house as social architecture

Domestic space is designed as a space of social and cultural inscription structured by the collective and symbolic organization of its residents (Bachelard 1969:14). The structural oppositions inscribed in this space match those traversing the domestic group (Bourdieu 1980, Hirschon and Gold 1982, Taylor 1990, Gudeman and Rivera 1990). Similarly, the social and cultural world is organized in terms of metaphors provided by the house's physical layout: 'In the house model a figure from the built world – with foundation, supports, and doors – is used to talk about and organize material practices . . . Through the model, physical houses are turned into economic centers, while economic units are realized as houses' (Gudeman and Rivera 1990:40).

Among uprooted people, remembrance of a past home does not escape this logic. This type of collective memory, however, entails a distinct meaning system: it fosters and reproduces a cultural identity estranged from its territorial basis. Remembering the house in which an uprooted culture originated and developed involves reversing history and sinking symbolic roots into a vanished human and geographical world. The remembered house is a small-scale cosmology symbolically restoring the integrity of a shattered geography. 'The reason members of a group remain united, even after scattering and finding nothing in their new physical surroundings to recall the home they have left, is that they think of the old home and its layout . . . Thus we understand why spatial images play so important a role in the collective memory' (Halbwachs 1980:130).

The past evoked in the following pages is not one re-created through historical work inscribed in a *literary* medium (see Yerushalmi 1982). Rather, the things of the past meticulously re-created here are those *experienced* in daily life, in the crowded intimacy of the most familiar objects and people,

28

those one sees on rising in the morning and on going to sleep at night. This remembered past is lodged in the monotonous repetition of the necessary acts of concrete experience. The memory that 'invents' it (Lewis 1975) and rewrites it is the product of this relentless repetitiveness. Yet this remembrance of concrete experience is structured in terms of two main fusing dimensions: domestic space and family time. Events are not remembered simply as they were experienced by the family and the domestic community. Memory draws the boundaries of the family and domesticity by shaping within them local, regional, and international events. The domestic and family world makes up the woof of remembrance, of memory. The house is 'inhabited' by memory. Remembrance is moulded into the material and physical structures of the domestic space.

Dar-Refayil's memories are designed as an architecture of memory. The biographies collected tell the personal and collective history of Dar-Refayil's residents from 1937, when the Senoussis arrived in the house, until 1962, when most Jewish residents left for Algiers and then for France. Narratives significantly focus on the descriptions of the domestic life, with special emphasis on female accounts because women spent most of their time at home. These narrative memories provide a great many details on the layout of apartments, household accommodations and furnishings, the rhythm of daily life, eating, sleeping, bodily hygiene, and even sexual activity. At the outset, Dar-Refayil's memories seem to be confined to this enclosed world.

Then, as in Impressionist painting, a marked outward movement emerges. The mental reconstruction of the house proceeds by drawing successive narrative boundaries in the form of concentric circles radiating outward from the courtyard. These circles actually indicate the breadth of residents' social life. Starting from a nucleus comprising the rooms lined up around the courtyard, a sort of womb whose only opening is the house's heavy wooden gate, Dar-Refayil's people go out to participate in the city's multicultural life and in that of the Jewish community. They take part in movements of population that lead them to cities such as Constantine and Algiers to seek their fortunes. Narratives present residents' experiences as if they originated in the courtyard, in the heart of the house – as if the house were a spring from which all personal peregrinations and itineraries flowed. Dar-Refayil's domestic community, though confined in the house's protective enclosure, seems at the same time open to urban life and regional events. This dual nature of the domestic community – both exposed and protected – is apparent in the very structure of the narratives. It reveals the contradictory motives of the former residents, who valued domestic conviviality highly and were at the same time irresistibly attracted by the display of the European lifestyle. Memory transforms the house into the symbolic miniature of the Algerian social world. The remembered house is a sort of 'centre of the world'.

This narrative logic, opposing enclosure to opening, permeates the narrative description of the places – of the physical and social organization of domestic space.

The logic of enclosure

Doors and windows without a view

It is in no way surprising that, in this Maghrebian cultural world, memory's discourse feminizes the house grammatically even though the Arabic word *dar* designates the house of the father and of his lineage. Domesticity is described as an enclosure of feminity, a mother-house symbolically associated with reproduction. The architecture of the building, traditional in Maghrebian urban societies, above all allows and encourages the physical control of women. Consequently, what female memories retain most powerfully is the organization, the detailed layout, and the material equipment of this enclosed world, as if all these things had been addressed specifically to them. The young Madeleine who arrived in the house with a fervent desire for emancipation could not have responded positively to the passage from an open and promising society (represented in the material layout of a high-rise apartment building) to an enclosed domestic world. Dar-Refayil's female memories feminize this enclosure of domesticity because women knew that it was a message for them to internalize.[1] When recalling their neighbours in the house, my female interlocutors identified each family by the mother's first name: 'Nonna's family was in this room, Anna's lived in the apartment upstairs.'

The importance of the theme of enclosure is articulated by the recurring references to doors and windows in domestic memories. Early on in each interview I asked for a material description and a sketch of the house, and this would inevitably begin with the placing of doors and windows. In Dar-Refayil, as we have seen, all the doors and windows except those of the owners' apartment opened onto the courtyard. Given this structure, the domestic group could enjoy openings only onto itself; its mental and social perspective was entirely self-directed. Yet some exceptions to this rule appear in memories. Individual rooms on the ground floor were laid out differently from those on the first floor. Upstairs, two apartments – that of the Senoussis and that in which Anna Akoun and her children lived

– included several adjacent rooms. This is the reason that Dar-Refayil's former residents called these units 'apartments' as opposed to the 'rooms' of the lower floor. In both of the upstairs apartments, each room had two doors: one opened onto the balcony running around the second floor and overlooking the courtyard, the other into the next room. Residents of the ground floor interpreted additional openings as superior status: more openings meant more comfort. The spatial and social distribution of doors and windows reflects a minor hierarchy within the domestic community. Those whose apartments had more openings were viewed as higher on the social ladder. Similarly, the owners, who were the only residents to have a view onto the street, were considered the only ones with symbolic access to the town's European community. Doors and windows were a metaphor for an open society; they embodied the desire for social advancement.

Reference to enclosure is ambiguous: it either emphasizes the space's hermetic closure or highlights its internal openness. Memory wavers between openness and enclosure in evoking the domestic space. In this oscillation, memory's discourse reverses itself: the lack of windows opening onto the street becomes a metaphor for the ghettoization of the domestic group and the stifling of the individual. At the same time, the permanent openness of all interior doors is interpreted as giving conviviality and security:

We always left the doors open. We never closed them. and that's why we lived like one big family. If a neighour needed anything, she just came in; she didn't need to knock. Here [in France], house doors are closed, but there [in Sétif] all the doors were open. From morning, when we got up, we left the doors open till evening, when we closed them before going to bed. We'd go to the market, we'd leave our doors open, and at night, we closed them with a little bolt; you could open the door with your finger. So we lived as one family, not just as neighbours, and we had a good life, we really had a good life.   *(Clarisse)*

Dar-Refayil is here portrayed as what Bachelard calls a 'felicitous space' (1969:xxxi). This 'topophilia' (Bachelard 1964: xxxi; Tuan 1974:93–99) inscribed in the discourse of memory operates as a defence of family values as the *moral* values of the domestic group. Familism is here objectified through an architectural metaphor – a semantic procedure widespread in Mediterranean and European cultures (Herzfeld 1987:203–4). At the same time, the narratives reveal the ambiguity of these values in a society seeking emancipation. Familism is comfortable as long as it does not interfere with the individual's attempts at social advancement and integration into local society:

It was a bit of a mess, communal toilets, doors which wouldn't close, spiders and cockroaches all over. It was really awful.   *(Guy)*

There were lots of windows, but with no view . . . all looking onto the courtyard. Doors were bits of cardboard, there weren't even locks. So you can imagine what it was for newlyweds . . . no door, just a little curtain to screen them.   *(Rosette)*

Open doors represent conviviality and good life but also lack of privacy: an open door may be either positive or negative. This oscillation recurs in the comparison between life at Dar-Refayil and life in France. In France doors are closed, and there is little conviviality or mutual help, but at the same time there is a sense of privacy and a better material life. While Setifian life is remembered as communally oriented, French life is viewed as individually oriented. In several narratives, in particular those offered by the residents with the lowest incomes, the symbolic opposition between open and closed is associated with that between clean and dirty. For Guy Bakoushe, a closed door means that light and air cannot come in; it is a sign of social and cultural suffocation. For an adolescent in the fifties, eager to discover the world, doors shut in dirt, impurity, and social backwardness.

Ultimately, narratives translate the opening of doors and windows onto the courtyard rather than the street as the enclosure of the domestic group, a sort of metaphor of endogamy materially represented by burdensome overcrowding and lack of privacy and by the clutter of domesticity.[2] Doors and windows are used metaphorically in narratives with a logic different from that of Proust's *Remembrance of Things Past*. In Proust windows give access to individual secrets, operating as narrative spies (Moss 1962:43).[3] By contrast, the opening of Dar-Refayil's doors and windows is associated with its domestic group's social opening outward – in a sense, towards the future. Narratively, the house's interior represents the past and social backwardness, the outside the future and social advancement. Closed doors are interpreted as the visual expression of entrenched archaic traditions and social stagnation. By contrast, doors are opened to social and cultural progress. As in Edward Hopper's paintings, the windows of narrative memory open onto dreams of social and material achievement. When they talk about windows, Jewish women specifically invest this metaphor with their ideal of female and general autonomy. Their memories visualize Muslim women perpetually behind closed doors and windows and thus in social misery. For these Jews who were teenagers in the fifties, doors and windows are full of promise. The narration of their uprooted lives in the eighties reveals in great detail how they managed to break down the barrier of closed doors and windows. Their voices now resonate from the other side of those barriers. These doors and windows are narrative metaphors for the frontiers – geographical, social, and cultural – that were crossed in reality in the great migration.

The individual confined

In Dar-Refayil, families of five to eight persons lived in rooms of just over ten square metres, which served as bedrooms, kitchens, washrooms, and living rooms. For families that only had one room, the whole of domestic life had to take place in this restricted space. Therefore each domestic activity had to be differentiated by reserving a distinct *corner* for it. Thus Khaddouj is said to have set up a kitchen in a storage area[4] of her unique room. The dwellings around the courtyard were all much smaller than those on the upper floor. The overcrowding was much more oppressive around the courtyard: inferiority is thus a material metaphor used in narratives at two levels of signification, physical and socio-material. As a result, there were more Muslim families on the ground floor, whereas only Jewish families occupied the apartments of the upper floor. Some Jewish families rented scattered single rooms: the Bakoushes, for example, used a room on the upper floor as their bedroom and a room on the ground floor as their kitchen. In a way, the Bakoushes' status was thus intermediate between the privileged and the underprivileged. Translating their liminal position, their neighbours ironically commented on their movements within the house, comparing them to the seasonal migrations of royal families: 'They had a winter palace and a summer residence', said the women.

Overall, population density in Dar-Refayil was overwhelming, especially when it came to bodily activities such as hygiene, sex, and sleep. Memories represent the individual body as being swallowed up by the collectivity, by the cramped space and its odours. The individual was absorbed, but the bodily was everywhere, encroaching, obstructing.

Two themes related to physicality are often mentioned in the recollection of this overcrowding: that of the wandering sleeper or the migrant mattress, and that of unconcealed sexuality. In the most destitute or the largest of families, mattresses accumulated as successive children were born and grew up. Restricted space did not allow each family member to sleep in the same separate bed every night. Children's mattresses were spread out on the floor, leaving one bedroom available for the parents. As the oldest sons married, according to patrilocal tradition, they settled in the groom's parents' household and were given, for the time being, the 'nuptial room', as the women called it – a space reserved for conjugal fertility and equipped with a raised bed. Women say, 'When you got married, you *climbed onto a bed'*; you no longer slept on the floor. This metaphor of high and low sleeping is clearly related to the status of individuals within the family and the domestic community. Those who slept on the floor and those with migrant mattresses were of lower status. Thus eldest brothers always slept on single beds and not on mere mattresses, leaving their younger sisters to sleep on the floor on movable mattresses. Some girls preferred to spend a night at an aunt's, not far from their parents' home, from time to time. Aimée was unlucky enough to be born just as her older brothers were getting married and settling with their wives in the room with the raised bed. For a while, Marcel and Eddie occupied the two bedrooms as newlyweds, and Aimée wandered around with her bedding: 'You never had the same place. You slept here or you slept there. One never had the same bed. I slept anywhere, wherever there was a bit of room.'[5]

The peregrinations of female bedding correspond to the women's peregrinations within the community and to their status in this strongly patriarchal family. Time and again, narratives use a material metaphor to signify a social pattern. A stationary bed corresponds to power within the family; a movable bed to weakness and submission. Despite space constraints, the organization of sleeping space followed the rules of the separation of bodies by sex as much as possible. Until the age of puberty, it was a matter of indifference where in the home children slept. Boys and girls both slept next to their parents or all in the same room. Later on, brothers and sisters might sleep in the same room but would share different double beds according to their sex. In some cases, a single divan was purchased for the oldest boy in his late teenage years. Under these conditions, conjugal sexuality was encumbered by the household's crowdedness. During periods in which two married brothers were living at home with their wives, young couples had no sexual privacy. Women's amused narratives evoke this atmosphere by making the night sound like a soccer game: 'So Eddie made love at such-and-such a time . . . All three of us [Moushi, Eddie, Marcel, and their wives] made love at the same time. We cried out together. It was as if a signal had been given, as if the whistle had been blown. One could hear the beds, which were old. That's the way we were, living on top of each other' (Rosette).[6]

The theme of the wandering sleeper indicates the social fragility of the domestic community. It is as if a breakdown, a conflict latent in the apparent domestic conviviality, were imminent. This wandering appears in the narratives as an omen of forthcoming departure, migration, and social fragmentation. It also highlights the mobility of these large households: new children are born as older ones get married and have their own children. Some children are leaving as others are arriving. Generations criss cross in the genealogical order. It was women who moved the most in this inner mobile world. The home was their universe, where most of their social experiences took place, yet within this world they had no stability. They were always on the move – between different rooms in the same apartment, between different apartments when, for example, they married a neighbour. In women's memories, the domestic world is both a place of rootedness and enclosure and a place of instability and internal mobility.

Bodily hygiene was also subject to the constraints of this ambient lack of privacy. There were no washrooms in Dar-Refayil, and only kitchens were equipped with running water. Residents would draw water from a well or fountain in the courtyard near the main gate. One of the house's lavatories was also near this well or fountain, with the result that dirty and clean commingled. There were only two lavatories for all the tenants, and they were 'Oriental-style'[7] lavatories with no toilet or seat. Only the owners' apartment was equipped with what was known as an 'English' lavatory, revealing their social superiority. Materially, the designs of these two kinds of lavatories constituted a metaphor for the cultural hierarchy of 'Oriental' and 'European' in colonial ideology. 'Oriental' lavatories were used in a squatting position, close to the floor, whereas 'European' lavatories were used in a seated position on an elevated seat. The emphasis on this opposition in Jewish narratives points to the equivalent opposition between clean ('European') and dirty ('Oriental'), ultimately referring to the opposition between the self and the Other and revealing to which side of the Mediterranean these Jews directed their expectations and self-identification. The opposition between high and low lavatories recalls the opposition in sleeping styles just described.

Hygiene in Dar-Refayil was organized in terms of a structural opposition between daily life and festive occasions, but neither context offered the possibility of washing in private. Daily ablutions consisted in a wash using a copper bowl, the *kesa'a*, filled with heated water and placed in the middle of the kitchen space. There was no hot running water, since Dar-Refayil had no boiler. The daily wash was thorough for children, but adults would limit it to the private parts, the face, the armpits, and the feet. Some managed to achieve a bit of privacy by taking turns washing behind the kitchen door. In Jewish families the main bathing was done on Friday, just before the sabbath, at the *hammam*. Jewish memory significantly retains this scheduling of the clean versus the dirty by associating the former with ritual. In Dar-Refayil as in many other Jewish residences, one would never enter a ritual period without having washed thoroughly. Cleanliness was *sacred*. The body had to be clean before the sabbath and the main Jewish religious festivals, and the home had to go through similar purification: extensive house cleaning would take place on Thursdays or Fridays and also during the month preceding Passover. Before the Jewish new year, Rosh Hashana, new clothes would be bought for the children for their visit to the synagogue. The hygienic calendar was thus essentially religious and constituted a physical and ritual distinction between the confessional groups gathered in the house.

Nothing and everything

This house had many people but few amenities. Memory reports that domestic comfort was inversely proportional to the demographic density of the space. Claude insisted on this: 'There was nothing', no individual lavatories, no individual beds for some, no individual washroom for anyone, no central heating, no hot water, and no washing machine.[8] To perform all the practical activities of daily life required a complex and encumbered organization of movements. This is the metaphor conveyed by the memories of former Jewish residents who live today in comfortable French apartments equipped with everything they say they lacked in Sétif. Yet the statement 'There was nothing' is a product of temporal remoteness. The message is clear: there was no material wealth, but abundant conviviality made up for it. Human warmth is said to have overcome the difficulties of daily life: 'The ambiance and all was really good. We lived well. We had less . . . we did not have abundance and all like we we do now, but we had a better life there. Ah! It was great, there was a festive ambiance. We had everything – we had respect, we had everything, we had it all' (Eddie). What is the meaning of this abundance of 'nothing', contrasting with the 'everything' of human warmth? Why does the discourse of memory oppose lack and abundance as it does closure and openness? At first glance, narratives seem to be preoccupied with temperature.

Located at an altitude of 1,100 metres, Sétif is the capital of the high plateau of eastern Algeria. Winters are long and cold, snowfall not being unusual in March, and summers are very hot. Domestic adjustment to these seasonal changes was a constant worry in Dar-Refayil. The house was equipped neither with central heating nor with electric refrigeration. Refrigerators came to Dar-Refayil only in the last years before the exodus. Thus only non-perishable foodstuffs – cereals and grains, spices and dried herbs, vegetables preserved in brine or in vinegar, home-made fruit preserves, etc. – were stored at home. Meat, milk, and fresh vegetables were bought on a daily basis. In the summer, drinks and cuts of meat were placed for a few hours in a wide, deep basin containing big blocks of ice.

When referring to anything related to heat, whether heating or cooking facilities, memory consistently effects a transfer from the material to the social register. It is as if it were trying to compensate symbolically for the lack of material comfort with an abundance of emotion and conviviality:

> In the winter, we used the *kanoun* [three-legged clay brazier] for heating. We would all sit around it and tell stories. Our father, my mother would tell stories, as in traditional evening gatherings. We'd put a mattress on the floor, and we'd all sit on it, and he would tell stories – stories about days gone by, about his youth. My mother would tell us that she had become an orphan when she was very young . . . and that she had had typhus . . .   *(Zahra)*

Memory humanizes rather primitive material conditions; in this domestic world everything is socialized and communalized. Thus the use of cooking facilities and utensils was governed not only by limited possibilities but also by the social distinction between times, places, and people. The kitchen seems to have been a shrine to corporality: meals were prepared and sometimes eaten there, and daily ablutions were performed there. Even when the kitchen was just a corner of the one-room living space, every square metre of this area could be distinguished by the specific activities that characterized it. It was as if one made up for limited space by compartmentalizing – enlarging space by multiplying its material uses. Narratives sometimes suggest a chaotic muddle, but at the same time they convey quite clearly the sense of distinction and order that ruled the whole of daily life of Dar-Refayil.

Even cooking pots were socially differentiated. In the forties, Dar-Refayil cooks used charcoal stoves carved out of raised blocks of granite. Cooking pots rested on iron bars placed on top of the coals. Above the stove was a hood made of brick to allow cooking odours and grease to escape. The tediousness of this cooking technique and of the cleaning up of the ash it scattered around the room recur in many accounts. Kerosene stoves began to come into use in the early fifties; gas in cylinders, which made it possible to have 'cleaner' cooking areas, came only towards the end of the decade.

For heating, people used alternatively charcoal, kerosene, or gas. Each household had a charcoal stove for heating, either in the middle of its single room, or in its living room. A multi-room apartment also had a fireplace, but it was rarely used for heating except on very cold winter evenings. Instead, the fireplace was decorative: the mantlepiece held tablemats, knick-knacks, or copper plate pestles and trays bearing witness to the family's heritage.[9] The *kanoun* was an alternative method of heating and for some Muslim households the only one. In Jewish narrative an image stands out in recollections of the sabbath: several *kanoun* were set up on a corner of the cooking counter behind a thin curtain as a way of creating a rudimentary separation between the utensils used in everyday cooking and those reserved for ritual. In the Senoussi and the Akoun households there was even a different *kanoun* for each sabbath dish: 'one for the meatballs, one for the *t'fina*,[10] one for the couscous!' The *kanoun* is evoked as the practical embodiment of the return to native traditions which took place during the sabbath and the major religious festivals. Its image is a representation of a return to one's roots.

The distinctions made between the three types of heating and cooking constitute a narrative strategy for distinguishing between Jews and Muslims in the house. The basic lightweight and unsophisticated appliance placed on the ground (the *kanoun*) represents slow cooking, simmering dishes, and above all the socioeconomic stasis of colonized native people. Kerosene and gas, in contrast, represent easy, quick, modern cooking and a modern lifestyle, even a physical (and social) ascent, of which the eventual next step is the elevated gas stove.

Similarly, the cooking pots used for the sabbath were differentiated from other pots, but by nothing more than a curtain. In referring to this domestic organization, memory discriminates time sequences in the same way as the utensils that materialize them. The numerous evocations of the *kanoun*'s usage underline the way in which this little device at once distinguished Jews from Muslims and brought them together. Muslims used the *kanoun* in their daily cooking, whereas Jews made it the objectified representation of their religious festivals. In this remembered domestic life, the sacredness of Jewish festivals distinguishes the Jews from their Muslim neighbours while at the same time focusing on their shared indigenous culture. The curtain separating the cooking pots appears in memory as an entirely 'symbolic'[11] sign of distinction, an ironic one underlining how fragile this distinction really was.

What is the symbolic logic that causes memory to oscillate between powerful negative images and comforting images of lost domestic harmony – between openness and closure, dearth and abundance, cleanliness and dirt, hot and cold? Does uprooted Jewish memory embellish the past as Valensi and Wachtel (1991) seem to suggest? Is this narrative strategy a mere effect of nostalgia? It seems to me that in these structural oscillations memory expresses the constraints and contradictions of domestic existence. Narratives conceal nothing, whether pleasure or pain, about past domestic life, and these oscillations do not, in my judgement, alternate remembrance with forgiveness. Rather, the emphasis on dearth and the harshness of life is a device allowing similar emphasis on the extensive efforts people made to humanize an uncomfortable niche. It constitutes a strategy for turning those who survived those miseries into heroes. Thus the banishing of dirt becomes synonymous with a festive atmosphere: 'There was *sôl* back there; for Passover, everything would be polished. . . . *sôl* means a festive atmosphere, the odour of festival, everyone would make the house shine, *sparkle!*' (Clarisse). *Sôl* is a festive spirit that encompasses both the material and the human environment, and with it the narrative shifts from the oppressive image of dearth to the description of makeshift decorations or of opulent furnishings. Among these furnishings memory seems to have focused on sideboards, silver cabinets, and glass-fronted cupboards for displaying heirlooms. The few furniture items that families had were solid: 'Here, there was a solid wood wardrobe. In Algeria, there was no imitation furniture . . . The chairs . . . you'd sit comfortably in your chair' (Guy). The narrative here emphasizes the difference between the Algerian past and the French experience after emigration. In Algeria, domestic life was rudimentary and material possessions were few, but those few were better than the abundant items one could easily acquire in France. Time and again, one finds in this description of dearth the narrative reversal of negative to positive. What memory strives to generate in this alternation is the emphasis on the human dimension of coresidence. To have lived in Dar-Refayil becomes an adventure, a triumph. Narratives focus on the way people socialized dearth, closure, and lack of privacy. They constitute themselves as a lesson in humanity. Thus the oscillation between negative and positive is not nostalgia but a strategy for magnifying the ways in which coresidents transformed this cramped space into a liveable place.

The curtain: ironic separation

As we have seen, distinction was the rule in Dar-Refayil: individuals, families, religious groups, objects, areas, and times were all distinguished. However, one of the themes recurring most often in narratives is that of fusion, whether muddle or reunion. 'We were all mixed up together' and 'we lived on top of each other' were alternative ways of expressing both the spirit of fraternity and the crowdedness of the encumbered space. Here again, memory's discourse reverses itself.

Mixed up together Dar-Refayil's residents certainly were. Jews and

Muslims lived there side by side, several families sometimes shared a dwelling, and from time to time boys and girls slept in the same room. Narratives describe this blending sometimes as a muddle but most often as a happy arrangement, once again moralizing past life: was this internal harmony not remarkable while bombs were exploding outside and the town was shaken by war and discord? Were they not heroes to have been able to create harmony out of elements which elsewhere proved explosive?

Things and people were not in fact blended in this house, even though memories seem to present them as such. People made an effort to distinguish themselves from each other without thereby separating. As we have seen, a tenuous but complex social distinction was inscribed in the house's spatial organization. Socioeconomic differences between residents of the ground floor and those of the upper floor were tacitly recognized. To be downstairs around the courtyard meant being on the lowest rungs of the social ladder. At the very bottom of this hierarchy the discourse of memory placed those who had to sleep curled up on the floor. In colonial Algeria this sleeping position may have denoted a nomadic way of life and thus embodied the absolute opposite of a European lifestyle and the impossibility of emancipation. The owners occupied the top of this hierarchy, to the extent that they are said to have 'gone up' to their house. Remembrance places the Senoussis in an intermediate position; their apartment adjoined that of the owners, and it was also one of the two largest dwellings in the house. But above all they were the only tenants to whom the owners would lend their balcony for the celebration of life-cycle rituals. My explanation for the Senoussis' special status is that their extended family had been present in the house for quite a long time.

Needless to say, these differences in status overlapped with ethnic and religious differences: most Jewish families lived on the upper floor and all the Muslims below. And although they say that they lived in happy cohesion, these two groups were significantly differentiated on a daily basis. The semantics of remembrance traces several lines of distinction. To begin with, the owners had closer relationships with the Jewish families; they were Jewish, and their balcony was lent for Jewish rituals. In addition, since the end of the First World War, Jews and Muslims had no longer spoken the same language even though the Jews would occasionally communicate in Arabic. They did not use the same cooking utensils or have the same sort of furniture; European influences were more pronounced in Jewish households. When Jews celebrated their rituals on the balcony, they would hang a curtain around it in order, say the women, to respect their neighbours' religious beliefs and their privacy. This curtain constitutes a powerful sign of distinction in narratives. A thin curtain, indeed, a veil, separated objects of various uses, conjugal bedrooms, religious groups, and families: fragile, ironic separation that could only distinguish the *representations* of people, objects, groups, and bodies.

Whereas memory's reconstruction of Dar-Refayil is riddled with distinctions which it proceeds to transgress, it also attributes value to places where residents could meet. These include the balconied galleries running around the first floor rooms, the owners' balcony and the terrace on the roof, the laundry room, and the courtyard. The balconied galleries were above all a place of passage, but they are remembered as a place of relaxation: women revel in recalling the chats they had there with their female neighbours. Men viewed these ostensibly marginal places, possibly with envy, as the privileged space for female togetherness: 'Women stayed at home all day long, so they used to call on each other on the galleries. They went around to visit each other, to chat; they'd spend all day like that, together' (Claude). This very male picture of women leading a relaxed life devoted to chatting does in fact re-create one aspect of the way in which women socialized though closeted in the house: the galleries were the place for sharing information and exchanging goods and services. Galleries are described as an intermediate space between individual families and the domestic community as a whole. The extensive spring cleaning which Jewish women would do before Passover emphasized this status; as rooms were gradually cleaned, the galleries would be full of the furniture and people moved out to allow this. They were a place for communication between women and between families, and they were also considered the antechamber of ritual cleanliness – the spatial representation of the liminal time between two festivals and two kinds of domestic chores, between private and public, between the everyday and the sacred (Brandes 1990).

The courtyard: womb of the mother-house

As Bachelard has pointed out, 'A house is imagined as a concentrated being. It appeals to our consciousness of centrality' (1969:17). In Dar-Refayil's memories the courtyard has this symbolic status. It is remembered as the centre of the domestic community, as creating its bonding (Brandes 1975 and 1990). In Muslim accounts the community is called not *dar-* but *hart* Refayil, 'the Refayil district', and is associated with the courtyard (see Al-Messiri Nadim 1979). The starting point for all narratives is the courtyard, which is constructed as representing *togetherness*. Several different types of chores and exchanges took place in the courtyard. These were mainly performed by women, who remember the courtyard as a place of reunion and protection. Rosette, who moved into the house in 1949 following her marriage to Marcel, speaks of the 'girls of the courtyard' as if the courtyard belonged to them and they to it. The courtyard is the spatial framing of female identity, since women spent most of their time there. Viviane, Eddie and Clarisse's daughter, was born in the house in 1954 and spent her early childhood in the courtyard playing with other children and chatting with her Muslim female neighbours: 'In Sétif, I knew I could do what I wanted; the courtyard was there. I could go down whenever I wanted' (Viviane).

The courtyard protected children from the dangers of the street. Thus, along with women's work and conversation it sheltered little girls' games. In female memories it is clearly associated with motherhood. The courtyard assisted women in raising their children and in their maternal tasks in general. In some narratives it is an intermediate place between the street and the home, a symbolic extension of each. Its cobblestones were reminiscent of the discomfort of the street: 'You would twist your ankles going in!' says Rosette. At the same time, it had the soothing and convivial atmosphere of the domestic group. It was a collective space, a place for sharing. Jews and Muslims would chat and work there side by side; they would raise their children there together. Until the late forties Jewish women would do their weekly laundry there, in the laundry room near the old fountain. They would convene there every Sunday, summer and winter, and spend several hours scrubbing and rinsing. 'The washerwomen', as one calls them, recalling an eighteenth-century rustic painting, would place their coppers on trestles to boil the water. These Sunday washing sessions remain associated with the symbolism of enclosure and of sexual segregation in the domestic space.[12] It was cold in the courtyard in winter and working hands would spend hours in freezing water. While boys and young men were having a good time downtown with their friends, young women washed: it is in terms of this semantic contrast that the event has become fixed in women's memories. Yet the weekly washing was also a key moment in women's social life:

On Sunday we did the washing. Instead of going for a stroll, we did the washing, we hung the clothes out to dry. Then, after the clothes were dry, we'd darn and iron. That was our Sunday treat!   *(Madeleine)*

Esther would bake bread for us and serve it with tomato sauce, red pepper, and garlic. Also, she would serve some stale bread with *tshuktshuka* [sautéed tomato, pepper, and onion salad] and hot sauce. Everyone did a little bit [in providing snacks]. Or else we'd buy fritters. And we'd get together in the galleries. My father would send us some sausages. We'd have a break to eat, and then we'd all pick up our basins again. And there was the criticism, too: who had the cleanest laundry, the whitest . . . We'd say, 'Ooh! Look at her, she's dirty, her laundry's grey!' *(Yvette)*

Despite the critical gossip, women remember the washing sessions as an occasion for female togetherness and complicity in the face of their imprisonment by domestic chores:

We'd do our washing in the courtyard . . . the whole house, on Sunday. We'd chat, we'd spend wonderful days . . . even though we had tons of washing to do, all the women did . . . And we'd get along, except sometimes, little arguments over the children, you know what it's like in a courtyard.   *(Zahra)*

Around ten, our grannies upstairs would prepare a snack for us, sausages, a hot *djare* [mint-flavoured tomato and garlic soup] because we'd be cold. We had to do the washing in all weathers. So [they'd say], 'Today, it's your turn to hang out. After it dries, I'm next. You pick up your laundry and I lay mine out.' That was our life, a communal life, indeed a bit like a kibbutz.   *(Rosette)*

Apart from these memorable weekly washing sessions, women would also come together in the courtyard to prepare food for festivities and preserves for the winter. There they would pound salt,[13] spices, and dried peppers. Any cooking chores which could not be performed in the small, cramped kitchen were done in the courtyard. The beef trotters used in the sabbath dish were first grilled in the courtyard on a *kanoun*. Some families baked their matzos for Passover in the courtyard, dividing the work of kneading, flattening, and baking. Drawn by the smell of baking bread, children would come down when Muslim women were baking their daily *metlo'h* and *kesra* (breads made of finely ground semolina, the latter unleavened) and be the first to try some: 'As soon as she'd take the *metlo'h* out of the fire, she'd break it in two, and as it was all hot, I wanted to taste it, it smelled good. She'd give me a bite. I couldn't wait for her to break it and give me some' (Viviane). Every now and then, Muslim and Jewish women together would take up their places in front of their doors, sitting on low stools and chatting. In these memories, the courtyard is described as an extension of the privacy of the home. The crampedness of individual dwellings was made up for by the courtyard's openness: open to the elements, open to families to communicate, and open to children to play safely as well.

Memory sacralizes the courtyard. The drinking water from the well used until the installation of running water was considered propitious: 'Children would be given this water to drink. No one was ever ill from drinking it' (Yvette). In a corner of it there was for a long time a tree that provided shade on hot summer days, and it was believed to have beneficial powers. It was revered because the black Berbers, the Bou-Sa'adi, would come there to perform rituals against demonic possession: 'On special days, we'd wash it, we'd give it the *'ers*,[14] we'd put make up on it' (Yvette). Gilda was an expert in this cult of the magical tree. Having been initiated by Ma Sultana into the secrets of popular superstitions and magic, she would sometimes put magic potions at the foot of the tree to resolve a family crisis, including conjugal infertility, or to help cure a child of illness. The tree assisted her in her protection of families or of *the* family. The Muslims of the house and Muslims from elsewhere often asked for her (and the tree's) assistance. The tree was a link between religious communities, the focus of local beliefs they shared. It was a 'symbol', as Yvette says, of the many blessings protecting the house's residents and their families and of their good relationships with their neighbours. The tree protected the entire domestic group and provided it with prestige and respect in the local community.

The logic of openness: out to the city

The street: a masculine forum for difference

The interior of Dar-Refayil is viewed as feminine and as a world of conviviality and mingling. All the material details of the domestic arrangement speak to this blending, and when men talk about this interior they describe it as women's territory. Remembrance of the house clearly records this gender-based definition of the domestic space: remembrance of the space itself is gendered. Contrasting with the internal feminine harmony, the street asserts itself as masculine and violent. The passage between these two worlds, inner and outer, is a passage from one sexual world to another (Brandes 1980 and 1990; Bourdieu 1980; Herzfeld 1987; Hirschon 1978). Remembrance of street life is clearly dominated by male narratives. Men talk about what was their own territory and about their bravery in confronting this world of sharpened differences. Men's narratives mostly report on experiences *outside* the house shared with friends made *inside* it. Men carried the domestic world into the street and into town through the friendships they had developed in the house:[15] 'The girls always stayed at home, but we were always out and about. We'd come back from school and we'd go out again to play football' (Claude).

Yet this gendered nature of street life did not last beyond the Second World War. Jewish women had begun to work outside during the war, both out of financial necessity and because some men were away either at the European front or doing their military service in Algeria. Male control over women in Jewish families decreased during this period, giving women more freedom, more authority in domestic affairs, and more independence in their choice of careers. Women who entered the workforce during the war discovered the excitement of the street world and of social life outside the house. After the war they demanded more autonomy, especially in relation to their leisure activities. By the fifties the street was no longer a male preserve; Jewish women born towards the end of the thirties walked about the street, too, and enjoyed themselves there. Female recollections often mention the Rue de Constantine, lined with arcades and clothing shops, cafés, and terraces where they could meet their friends and chat for a while. These recollections also evoke the walks they would take to the Jardin d'Orléans, at the far end of the Rue de Constantine, on the opposite side of the Porte d'Alger and the Fontaine du Marabout. Their movements were no longer limited to a shuttle between home, school, and workplace.

However, the parts of the town which remain most vivid in women's memories are those associated in one way or another with domestic life and women's work in the house, as if the town began in the courtyard. These places include food stores, the market, the communal oven, the public bath, their aunts' and grandmothers' homes, and the homes of other relatives they often visited. To identify the status of any family in the town, women describe their living conditions: 'They were ten to a room' means 'They were poor.' In female narratives, domestic life is used time and again as the identity marker for families. They describe best the dwellings of the Cité Lévy, a residential complex built in 1932 with funds provided by a local Jewish philanthropist. There, families lived in private houses which differed from Dar-Refayil in their individual layouts and their greater comfort. Women also talk about the 'posh' apartment buildings of the Rue d'Aumale, with individual family apartments, private bathrooms, and kitchens. In their narratives, collective residence is associated with the lowest social status, whereas separate residence, all things considered, means wealth. The world of the street is codified by social markers found in the domestic system.

Whereas women's remembrance of the street order is governed by their domestic experiences, men's memories emphasize their identity as residents of the the town. They talk about the 'Setifian' identity they developed through their socializing in the street. Thus, despite the disadvantages of life in this small town, where the opportunities for social advancement were few, and despite the fact that he was born in Tébessa, Guy Bakoushe introduces his narratives with the assertion of his Setifian identity:

I wasn't born in Sétif, but I feel I belong there because I grew up there. I was very young [when I came], only four or five. I would be on the side of a Setifian rather than a Tebessian. Only my younger brother was born in Sétif. They [my parents and older sisters] say they're Tebessian, but I am from Sétif. I grew up there.

On summer Saturdays, nobody was in the streets. It was so hot that the tar would run in the gutters. So all the children [of the house], we'd get together, we'd go bare-foot, we'd go wild. And when I'd return after fooling around, the soles of my feet were all black, covered with tar, because of the heat. But I do feel Sétif was very beautiful.

Guy spent most of his adolescence in the Setifian street with his friends from Dar-Refayil. In an account echoing his, Elie Akoun, born in Sétif in 1937, enjoyed telling me his Setifian dreams:

I left Sétif when I was twenty-five. You know what it's like to leave your country. When you go, you leave behind places where you built your life. To this day I dream about Sétif. In my dreams I walk again along the Rue de Constantine under the arcades, and it makes me feel happy . . . and then I wake up.

The Setifian street as remembered by men is essentially plural in charac-ter: masculine movements there are framed by emphatic religious and ethnic distinctions. Whereas the house is described as a harmonious and cheerful mingling, the multiethnic encounter in the street is said to have been violent.

Sétif was a walled town until the French arrived in the middle of the nineteenth century. Gates in the wall opened onto the roads to Algiers to the west, Bougie to the north, Constantine to the east, Aumale to the south-east, and Biskra to the south. To the north lay the old military quarter flanked by the Arsenal. To the south of this district, the Rue de Constantine, officially called Avenue Georges Clémenceau, crossed the town from east to west and divided it into two socio-geographic areas: the European area to the north and the indigenous, multiethnic area, which included a large commercial quarter, to the south. At the eastern end of this avenue lay the town hall and the mosque, and towards the back of the square were the synagogue and the Protestant church, built symbols of local ethnic and religious diversity. At the western end of the Rue de Constantine sat the high school, also known as Lycée Albertini or the boys' Lycée, which embodied French cultural domination. To the east, then, religious particularism was dominated by French political power; to the west stood the symbol of the ruling culture.

It was in the district of small shopkeepers, craftsmen, and workers south of the Rue de Constantine that Dar-Refayil stood, at the eastern end of the Rue Valée, which began opposite the Lycée. Though neighbours, ethnic and religious communities here were significantly distinguished. The gap between Europeans and the indigenous populations was wide, especially in the period between the end of the First World War and Algerian independence – a period marked by a significant population boom and the rise of several important political movements. Colonialist and racist ideologies and groups continued to proliferate amongst the European population as Algerian nationalism grew. Virulent anti-Semitism produced a profound separation between Jews and their Christian 'compatriots' (Ayoun and Cohen 1982:134–9; Bahloul 1987:24) and forced the Jews back to their 'native' origins alongside the Muslim population. Despite their strong desire for Frenchification and emancipation, the Jews of Sétif, like those of other Algerian small towns (see Friedman 1988 and Bel-Ange 1990), remained on the margins of European society. In the Jewish memories of Dar-Refayil, the Christian anti-Semitism in the Algeria of the time contrasts with the cordiality of their relationships with local Muslims. This three-sided game of ethnic pluralism was embodied in various domains of urban life.

Children's games

Sétif's urban pluralism was less a matter of geographical and physical boundaries than one of social, cultural, and political ones inscribed in the most trivial movements and interactions of daily life. Ethnic distinction in colonial Sétif was a system of flexible strategies (Barth 1969): the boundaries between ethnic groups were fluid and constantly adjusted to the contingencies of the successive wars. Dar-Refayil's men have been the more profoundly affected by these demarcation lines for having grown up in the street and established their identities in this hostile world. In the street, boys' games acted out these interethnic antagonisms. Guy Bakoushe described this climate by referring to the 'feisty' attitude of Jewish kids. His own father had introduced him to this overtly quarrelsome spirit by encouraging him 'not to let himself be pushed around, not to let people step on his toes'. Until the fifties, Sétif's Jews were a buffer between the Christians and the Muslims. Anti-Semitism had been increasing since the early twentieth century (Ayoun and Cohen 1982:134; Bahloul 1987:25; Dermenjian 1983). Algerian Jews had been granted French citizenship in 1870 and had taken part in both world wars in the French army.[16] They had gradually been integrated into the French school system, in which they had invested their hopes for social and professional advancement. Their enthusiasm as greenhorn Frenchmen had been dampened neither by the virulent interwar anti-Semitism nor by the status assigned to the Jews by the Vichy regime, which barred them from French schools after 1942.

Adolescents of the fifties such as Guy Bakoushe and Claude Senoussi had to face a daily struggle to be accepted as full-fledged Frenchmen in local European society:

There was this terrible separation between Jews and Catholics[17] in Sétif. There was a barrier. We didn't get along, Jews and Catholics. Therefore we didn't socialize with them, except in high school. I had some Catholic friends, but they were said to be anti-Jewish. We never had normal contacts with them as happens here in France. There were fights all the time between youngsters. When someone would say 'Dirty Jew!', Charlie B. and I would go in there . . . we'd always be the first [to react].   *(Guy)*

Of this triangular Christian–Jewish–Muslim logic young men who grew up in the street remember mainly the Christian racism and anti-Semitism, which they contrast with their friendly relationships with Muslims, especially those living on their side. Here is how Eddie describes this system in reporting on a chance encounter, in France, with a former Setifian Christian:

He said, 'Come on, let's have a drink together.' I answered, 'So now we drink, but before, we didn't drink together!' He said, 'Come on, that's all over now . . . We left everything in Algeria, the farms . . . !' Before, when the Arabs talked about colonialism, it was *them* [the French], the colonists. I said, 'All this is because of colonialism.' So he said, 'Are *we* the colonists?!' I said, 'So who? *You* were the ones who did all that! *We* [the Jews] got along with the Arabs. From time to time, *you*'d set them against us.' They'd egg them on with money.

Jews remember Judaeo-Arab discord before the war of independence as mainly provoked by French anti-Semitism. Children's games strikingly reflect this 'social drama' (Turner 1974). The two communities then held different positions in the social and political landscape. Jews were closer to European society even though most of them were excluded from it; they were perceived by Muslims and saw themselves as superior. Though most Jews were close to Muslims in domestic life and through cultural affinities, they would take opposite sides on the street, as Claude explains:

Back there, we were friends in the classroom, we'd have fun. But as soon as we were outside, each went their own way: Christians on one side, Jews on the other, and Arabs on another side. When we'd meet in the street, we'd talk to each other, but we wouldn't go out together, to the movies at night for example. When we'd play football on a vacant lot, we'd always play Jews against Arabs. And it often ended in a fight, because if we'd win [they would feel offended]. There were some suburbs, shantytowns, where only Arabs would live, and we didn't know these Arabs. So they'd come, they'd see us playing. It usually ended in a fight. They'd kick us during the game, they'd call us 'dirty Jews!', (*l'yehud* in Arabic). But this had nothing to do with war. It was just children's quarrels!

Outside the city

Travel was not a customary leisure activity among Dar-Refayil's people. Travel out of town, for professional, business, or educational reasons, was more common amongst the local Jewish middle class. For Dar-Refayil's residents leaving town meant leaving the house to seek one's fortune in the city, usually Algiers. Geographic mobility was thus generally concomitant with upward social mobility. Thus Elie left Sétif for a few years to study dentistry in Algiers. He came back occasionally to visit his parents, especially for religious holidays, but when he graduated in 1961 the time had already come for him to leave Algeria altogether. Eddie got a job in the hospital in Bordj-Bou-Arreridj when he quit working in his father's butcher shop, but this was only a provisional move: the regular shuttle between Sétif and Bordj had become dangerous since the beginning of the war of independence. Moreover, returning to Bordj, which his father had left after the First World War because of unemployment, could not be associated either symbolically or practically with the social advancement for which Eddie had abandoned his father's business.

Peregrinations that memory traces back in geography foreground how vulnerable Sétif's Jews were, both socially and economically. Dar-Refayil's residents never took vacations at seaside resorts or in the countryside, and when they visited relatives out of town it was always to celebrate a birth or a wedding. Thus Moushi and Gilda went to Algiers in 1946 to join in the rejoicing at the birth of their first grandchild, Reine, Madeleine's daughter, taking with them prepared dishes and a roast lamb sacrificed for the occasion.

From time to time, the boys in the house would go to Constantine to attend the Talmud Torah classes of that pious city. Similarly, on one of her few pleasant trips out of the house, the young Clarisse accompanied her elder brother to Hammam Guergour, a village near the Guergour Springs, known for their medical virtues (especially for the treatment of rheumatism), about seventy kilometres northwest of Sétif. While her brother underwent treatment during the day, Clarisse stayed in the little rented studio and prepared their meals. Even though she was doing very much the same thing as she did in Dar-Refayil, she was happy to leave the domestic fold to enjoy an illusory independence.

The limited scope of Jewish memory in describing the surrounding countryside is in my view linked to two major historical processes. On the one hand, it shows that this vulnerable community was already in motion in the period in question. Although many of these Jews speak nostalgically about Sétif, they show no great attachment to or affection for the surrounding landscape. The spirit which feeds their memories is a deracinated one, one which they fill with dreams of remote and promising lands rather than with laments for a lost homeland. Their remembered Algerian travels usually took them to places where they had family contacts, as if the domestic microcosm stretched beyond the house along the social structures provided by the domestic group. The travels of Dar-Refayil's residents were circumscribed by this social space.

3

Telling people: the house and the world

The memory of domestic space is not simply a nostalgic sketch of a house from the past. As we have seen, its shape is defined by the social structures and relations of the resident group. The memory of the domestic space is that of the experience of dwelling. If the description of the domestic space has meaning it is because it is the lived representation of a social and mental world. Dar-Refayil was a 'house' in the anthropological sense of the term (Lévi-Strauss 1987a), and as such memory retrieves it: it functioned as a hierarchical system of relationships, exchanges, and obligations. As in other 'house based' societies, its residents had come to perceive it as 'a moral person, with . . . both material and immaterial properties' (Lévi-Strauss 1987c:34, my translation). The ethnography and history of Mediterranean societies have clearly established the mechanisms by which such domestic groups operate. In southern Europe (Assier-Andrieu 1987; Aymard 1977; Balfet, Bromberger, and Ravis-Giordani 1976; Collomp 1978; Herzfeld 1991a; Hirschon 1978 and 1989; Hirschon and Gold 1982; Lamaison and Claverie 1982; Rogers 1991; Wylie 1957) and in the southern Mediterranean (Geertz 1979, Munson 1984, Bedoucha 1987) the house and the domestic group are social units that define community organization, the forms of social exchange, the inheritance system, and the transmission of knowledge. The house is a social entity defined above all by kinship ties and obligations. The Jewish societies that developed within this sociocultural context modelled their organization on similar structures which offered flexibility but were solidified by the dense fabric of family groups (Goitein 1978). In addition, as Geertz (1979) has clearly shown, the boundaries of the Maghrebian domestic group are not simply genealogical; the group also includes relationships of neighbourhood, friendship, and personal affinity which have been incorporated into it simply because they evolve within the domestic world. Eventually, as Dar-Refayil's memories powerfully demonstrated, these domestic relationships may well become kinship ties through the matrimonial alliances between neighbours that they facilitate and encourage. Thus the structural model at work in narratives is that of the family.

On the surface, the past world remembered by Dar-Refayil's men and women is re-created in terms of two narrative principles: family and neighbours. In reality, the two categories usually overlap: neighbours are incorporated into the kin group, and some relatives are treated and designated simply as 'neighbours'. For example, Little Mouna to this day takes part in the Senoussis' and the Akouns' reunions even though she is in no way related to either. More interesting for our purposes is the overlapping of the categories of family and neighbourhood entails an ideological strategy in the narrative structure of Dar-Refayil's memories. The remembered domestic world unfolds as a discourse on pluralism and union, on the family and its bonds, on the economic adjustment of low-income people, and, finally, on the solidity of neighbourhood ties seen as kinship ties. Dar-Refayil's memories are both *a* family story and family *stories*. The house is a family house, and the family described takes on the material shape of the house. Memory merges the categories of family and neighbourhood:

I did not know who was my mother's sister or her sister-in-law. To me they all were relatives; they all belonged to the family. Take Irène and Denise [Little Mouna's daughters]: for a long time I thought they were relatives, my mother's sisters, because we all lived together, as a family.   *(Viviane)*

In reality, the notion of 'family' does not correspond to the large kin group it appears to be in memory. In Dar-Refayil there were only nuclear families or, rather, limited extended families. Individual households were sometimes composed of parents, their unmarried children, and one or more households of married sons. One would socialize with cousins, uncles, and aunts only if they lived in the house or very close by. It was *coresidence* in the domestic community that created family ties. Memory has recorded these as such, identifying everyone in the house as an assimilated relative, a classificatory kinsperson. For example, Ma Sultana was the second wife of Anna Akoun's father-in-law and lived in a room next to the Akouns' apartment. Everyone called her Mémé (Granny), and she was the universal grandmother:

Like all grandmothers, she was very kind, and we really liked to visit her because she'd give us lots of little gifts. We were young, we didn't understand. For us a sweet was a lot. And she was also the kind of grandmother who was always looking after her grandchildren. Her door was always open. She was a grand-mother to the entire house. She was everything for the house.   *(Clarisse)*

Anna, a grandmother herself, is remembered as the ideal mother. Her eldest son had settled with her after his marriage and his father's death. While her daughter-in-law Zahra was at work, Anna raised her grandchildren, who called her 'Mom'. Anna and Ma Sultana appear in the narratives as the human embodiment of the maternal model of which the house is the material representation. Together they represent the mother-house. The biological family has little relation to this notion of the family house. The house/family pair actually limits biological kinship to its most frequent and most immediate usage, living together. Coresidence brings unrelated people together, blending them into a symbolic world of all-inclusive kinship through its practical function and the daily experiences it entails.

As they revisit the house, Dar-Refayil's memories cross and transgress blood ties. The description of the house represents an ideal of cohesiveness, serving as the material support of memory's ideology. Yet at the same time this ideal is belied by the meanders of remembrance. Our narrators want to testify to the good family life that unfolded in Dar-Refayil, but their accounts reveal how personal itineraries gradually eroded family ties and ultimately led to a father's death. Remembrance of family life in Dar-Refayil is sad, nostalgic, and almost funereal in tone. It emphasizes the dilemmas these men and women had to face in their struggle to advance socially and to support large households. As we shall see, these dilemmas eventually led to the downfall of the family and its powerful values. Two key processes are blamed for this failure: the economic vulnerability of the Jewish families of Dar-Refayil and the irreversible dissolution of the family as a unit of production and consumption. In our narrators' accounts, these processes are evidenced by young people's access to work and women's access to economic autonomy in the post-war period.

Mother-house or father's house?

As in the Arab-Muslim communities of the Maghreb, the structure of the Jewish family in Sétif was patriarchal and patrilineal. Family authority and identity were transmitted through the patriline. Yet by the thirties this seemingly solid structure was beginning to erode. Paternal authority and the agnatic system were unable to withstand for very long the clear socioeconomic weakness of Jewish families. It was the absence of capital accumulation and financial security that led young people to leave the house, the town, and their families for the city and ultimately for France.

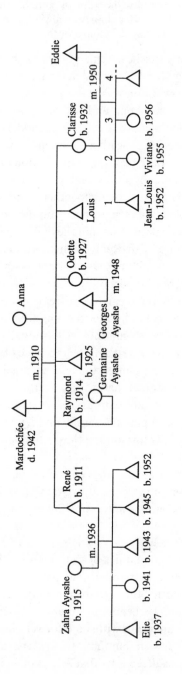

Figure 3.1 The Senoussis until 1961 (genealogy)

Both personal and professional biographies reflect this dilemma: choosing between a happy but not too comfortable conviviality and abundant but solitary fortune.

Dar-Refayil's memories emphasize the risks inherent in the traditional family's very structures. They tell us how this haven of peace was gradually torn apart by its inability to cope with the wave of emancipation in which young people of the interwar period were inevitably involved. It is this vulnerability that memory is talking about when it embellishes and hero- izes the family of the past. Even after their departure for France, the father's authority was never challenged by the guilt-ridden sons and daughters who one by one left the house and the father bemoaning his failure. This nostalgic lament for a vanished family is nothing but rhetoric asserting its vulnerability. Dar-Refayil's memories are permeated with a sense of family set up as an ideological model even in the narratives of those whose lives were damaged by it. No one questioned the father's authority, the respect due to him, or, above all, the power of the agnatic line. Women speak of it in terms of retrospective rebelliousness and filial affection.

Moushi was both authoritative and revered as a father, although he lost some of his power through his grief over his first wife's death. All his chil- dren recall his gentleness, honesty, and sacrifice for his family:

My father never let us go without new clothes for a holiday. He wouldn't dress up, but he never forgot us. He was a good father. He took more care of his children than he did of himself. He wasn't selfish. He did everything he could to pamper his children.   *(Claude)*

I always visualize my father looking the same; I always have the same image of him in my eyes: short, dark-haired, with a moustache. I was his favourite, so people say. I didn't realize this. It's because I was the last child, so he'd pamper me more than the others.   *(Aimée)*

He only ever thought about us, about his household. No one could say or do any- thing against his children. He was good to me, he wanted to keep me with him; he didn't want me to go to Algiers. He always tried to keep me close to him.   *(Eddie)*

I remember him as a saint. He was so kind! In the morning, he'd get up early. We wouldn't see him go. Everybody was sleeping when he'd go. He'd go to the shop to do some work, and then he'd come back. He'd wake us up around seven and bring us hot fritters, every morning. He was a wonderful father, always joking and laugh- ing.   *(Madeleine)*

The aura of saintliness in Madeleine's description of her father's per- sonality is no mere description of his character. At the time, Jewish father- hood was a structural pattern usually associated with the religious register, religious education, and religious ritual. The father was defined as the kinsperson in charge of the religious education given to a male teenager until his bar mitzvah[1] and sometimes beyond this. The bar mitzvah was a key moment in the public assertion of agnatic rule in Jewish families. Moushi was aware of this when he meticulously organized lavish celebrations for his sons. The dominant theme in Claude's and Guy's accounts of their bar mitzvahs is their entry into the order of agnatic authority. Among the details of the festivities, they both seem to remember best the role of paternal relatives:

I missed having my paternal grandfather at my confirmation, because he'd usually really pamper me.

(Guy)

Then there was Uncle S., my father's brother, who came from Algiers. So everyone was there!

(Claude)

In Guy's account the link between fatherhood and sacredness ended when his father died:

There was a time in my life, just before my father's death, when religion no longer meant anything to me. And, I tell you, I've never practised it since my father died. He died on the last day of Passover, and I even didn't celebrate Yom Kippur. Since my father's death, God has no longer existed. I said to myself, 'It's not possible that a forty-five year old man should just die like that, all of a sudden, stupidly.' I did not want to admit that my father had died so young. I had not had sufficient time to get the best out of him while I grew up, and I would have begun to do that at the age of seventeen. So when I became an adult, he vanished, and actually I always said that I missed my Dad all my life. I became bitter; I had to get even with God. I would stand outside the synagogue on Saturday morning and smoke in front of the people coming out, just on purpose.[2]

The fierce competition between father and God in Guy's recollections is a spectacular confirmation of the agnatic character of religious practise among Sétif's Jews as in other Jewish communities of the Maghreb. The father was respected as the kinsperson who introduced family members into the community of believers and the religiously literate. Some fathers performed this task strictly by carefully controlling the behaviour of their children and in particular that of their sons. Thus the rebellious Guy was often slapped for having dared to smoke on the sabbath. Men rationalized the ban on smoking as one aspect of the respect due to their fathers. They'd say: 'We wouldn't smoke on the sabbath out of respect for our father; smoking in front of him would have been an insult.' Through their respect for their father the sons respected the Jewish religion. In observing religious prescriptions, they practised a cult to fatherhood and asserted themselves to be the faithful descendants of a patriline of believers.

The structural ambiguity of all male narratives is that the father is represented as both an authoritative and oppressive figure and a complicitous and friendly one. It was the father who turned his sons into men – who taught them to be proud of being Jewish and male in the street and to struggle against fear. He is also remembered as a friend who shared and encouraged his sons' masculine pastimes. Above all, it was he who had exclusive control over the marriages of his children, sons and daughters alike. Overwhelmed by his family responsibilities, Moushi nevertheless exercised full authority over his sons' relationships with women. Rosette recounts her father-in-law's relentless activity in this matter:

He said, 'I want to marry my sons off while they're still young. As soon as they've begun to be interested in women, I'll get them married off. I don't want to see them fooling around. That's my only consolation: I'll marry them off.' That's what I always heard him say.

Fatherhood in Dar-Refayil could be fragile and short-lived, and several fathers died in their fifties or before. The family dynamics then quickly arranged the delegation of agnatic authority to firstborn males, whose authority among their siblings was unchallenged. Even if they followed a firstborn daughter, eldest sons enjoyed privileges and the respect of their younger siblings, especially their younger sisters, the structural juniors of the agnatic system. As we have seen, they were entitled to separate beds or, in some cases, a separate room, whereas other children would share mattresses and sleep on the floor. The Arabic terminology of address for eldest children is clear evidence of their superior status. Until very recently in the history of the Jews of Sétif, the eldest daughter was addressed as *lala* (Arabic for 'dame' or 'lady'), and the eldest son as *zeze* or *haze* (Arabic for 'my lord'). The authority of the latter increased when the father died. This is what happened when Anna Akoun lost a young husband in 1942, when her youngest daughter Clarisse was only a small child (see figure 3.2). Anna's eldest son, René,[3] had married in 1936, and his brothers and sisters looked on him as a father after their biological father's death. He established his household in Dar-Refayil close to his mother and siblings, and everybody saw him as a father-substitute, sometimes confusing him with Anna's brother. Clarisse describes this genealogical confusion as a strategy for family cohesion:

I was frightened of my eldest brother; even though he never scolded me, I was still frightened of him. And I never knew my father, so for me my eldest brother was my father. I called him 'Uncle René', and my younger brother did, too, but not the older boys. And Elie [René's son] also called his father 'Uncle René', since that's what we called him. And they called their mother 'Zahra'.

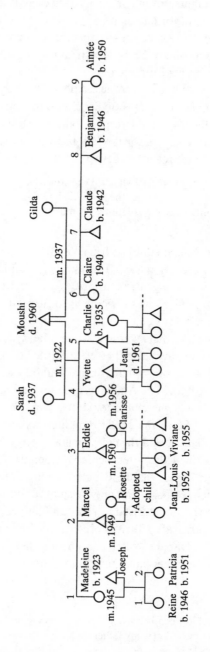

Figure 3.2 The Akouns (genealogy)

If the bar mitzvah was one key moment for the patriline's authority, the birth of the first grandson in the agnatic line was another. Thus the birth in 1952 of Eddie and Clarisse's first child Jean-Louis was one of the major events in Moushi's life after the birth of his own children. Marcel, Moushi's first son, had married Rosette in 1949, but the couple had had no children. The responsibility of ensuring the continuity of the Senoussi line therefore fell on Eddie. Moushi and Gilda worshipped Jean-Louis, who was the living embodiment of their success and the guarantee of its survival. As the first daughter-in-law to have ensured the patriline's reproduction, Clarisse too benefited from this special attention:

The day they were told it was a boy was a great joy for my father-in-law. He was the godfather. For him, Jean-Louis was a little god.[4] You really couldn't lay a finger on *his* Jean-Louis. If I punished him, he'd say, 'What have you done to him! You didn't have to hit him!' The first pair of shoes, the smart little suit would always be for Jean-Louis. Everything was for Jean-Louis. He spoiled him, maybe even too much. And then Jean-Louis was with him at home. I couldn't let him cry. They [Gilda and Moushi] were really nice to me.

The excessive attention that Moushi paid to his grandson was nourished by his sons' coresidence after their marriages. The rule in Sétif, as in the region as a whole, that newlyweds should live in the groom's father's home, observed until after the Second World War, allowed the agnatic lines to control the bride and the development of the new household. At the

Figure 3.3 Little Mouna's family (genealogy)

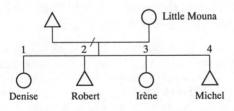

Figure 3.4 The Bakoushes (genealogy)

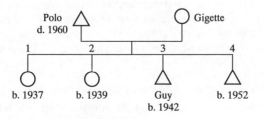

Senoussis', Moushi and Gilda gave up their conjugal bedroom to Marcel and Rosette in 1949. When the couple left the house for Algiers in 1950, and it was the turn of Eddie and Clarisse, married in 1950, to take over the famous 'nuptial room'. The narratives of daughters-in-law describe this overcrowding and lack of privacy as eventually leading to the erosion of family ties. Moushi's sons did not stay longer than a year or two in this father-dominated domestic group. Rosette was the best informant on this thorny subject:

For Jewish families in Sétif, it was a catastrophe when the children left. They could hardly even imagine this! Sons would never leave home, even if they were thirty and not yet married. We had brothers and uncles who were thirty and forty. They didn't get married, so they were still there, in their place at home, petted by Mom and Dad. Their socks were washed, their clothes ironed. And our husbands, too, they'd stay at home. It was unheard of that they'd leave and set up house on their own. It was unthinkable![5]

Patrilocality had various consequences for the organization of family budgets and domestic relationships, especially in the interactions between daughters-in-law and their parents-in-law. Women's memories, especially, reflect the lack of autonomy and financial dependence on their in-laws that they had to endure. Women's bodies, hygiene and culinary habits, and activities within and outside the home were under constant surveillance. When they entered the new household, often still as teenagers, after their weddings, the space available for everyone shrank, and the birth of babies made the situation worse. Parents had to keep finding extra corners for new members of a continually growing family. This crampedness is partic-ularly salient in Rosette's account of her first months in Dar-Refayil:

We were all sitting around the table for a meal – we were newlyweds – and one day I put my arm around my husband . . . Putting your arm like that was viewed as a bad gesture. Men would sit next to each other, and women would sit separately. My husband told me, 'The next time you put your hand around my chair like that, I'll slap you! I don't want my father to see you doing that.' We couldn't even kiss each other in front of our parents and parents-in-law. And well before my genera-tion it was even stricter. For me it was already loosening up a bit, but you still had to show respect. The bride would keep in the background when her parents-in-law were present. And we [brides] were dependent on them. We lived with them, so we had to live like them. If we ate soup, we'd eat it together, and from the same kitty. It was only one house. So then the second son would marry, the second daughter-in-law would come in; a room would be arranged for her . . . There were some con-flicts.

As the family grew and the domestic space shrank, family budgets grad-ually got smaller as well. There were economic limits to patriarchal and patrilocal rule. When Rosette came into the household in 1949, Marcel was working with his father in the small and unprofitable butcher shop supporting a family of ten. She hated to ask for her daily allowance for food purchases or for personal expenses: 'Even to buy a bra or panties, I had to ask my father-in-law!' Marcel was not paid a salary. Moushi handed over his daily takings to Gilda or Rosette every morning. As Moushi saw it, Rosette's personal expenditures were 'extras' in relation to the family's basic budget. None of his sons ever received any training beyond that which Moushi himself provided them in the shop. Occupations too were handed down from father to son in Sétif's Jewish community, and it was this system which eventually led to the breakup of this family whose only aim was to stay together. Although this highly patriarchal system was a burden for young married men, it is the daughters-in-law who express the most vivid awareness of this dilemma: their husbands were too deeply enmeshed in the structure of paternal authority to meet the basic needs of their wives and children even though, as family heads, they aimed to do so.

The image of fatherhood as it unfolds in Dar-Refayil's memories contains the reflection of a failed agnatic system. The father has control over the household budget and of every member's activities, but the seeds of his downfall lie in these very structures. Narratives elaborate Moushi's story as the embodiment of the dilemmas confronted by the agnatic system in Sétif before independence. In other households where the father had died he had quickly been replaced by the eldest son. Where there was no eldest son, as in the Bakoushe family, the family had left the house for an apartment. The paradox here is that domestic ideology and memory rest on a founding discourse whose axiom is motherhood, yet descriptions of domestic life portray a community dominated by paternal authority. The two sides of this discourse figure as the conflicting structures of Jewish society in prewar Algeria. The narrative begins with the death of a mother and the subsequent recovery of one; it ends with the death of a father and the scattering of the family.

Living from hand to mouth

'We lived from hand to mouth!' Young and old, Jews and Muslims, men and women all sum up their memories in this phrase, which seems to express their collective socioeconomic status and their common determination to survive in a threatening environment. It was this very vulnerability that brought Jews and Muslims together and made up the social cement of the domestic community. It is the women who most vigorously emphasize this hand-to-mouth lifestyle; they were the ones who managed family budgets dependent on scattered resources. It took ingenuity to make these limited budgets stretch beyond basic survival. As if to emphasize these past struggles, memory contrasts this aspect of the former domestic economy with the present pursuit of material possessions and profit. The narrative strategy consists in underlining the great sacrifices people made to arrive at this point:

> We didn't have the greedy spirit to say, 'We *have* to earn money!', like people today who say they have to scratch about, to do whatever they can to get money. We didn't think, 'Oh! If I have an extra buck, I'll put it aside for my old age.' No, we just thought about eating well today, about living decently, and starting again the next day. People didn't think about saving and investing money. It was rare for people to be obsessed with always having money in the bank. There were no savings banks. We didn't have this obsession we have today that you always have to have money and you'd be lost if you didn't. Instead, we aspired to happiness, and we were very happy as we were living the way we told you about.   *(Rosette)*

It is this same Rosette who described how difficult life was in Dar-Refayil – who related in detail the daily strategies for adjustment to dearth. In her memory as in the memories of other females, the description of the contents of shopping baskets and of clothing purchases serves as a practical imagery for measuring the status and wealth of each household. Resources are said to have been so scarce that households were unable to make financial plans for more than twenty-four hours at a time. Savings were impossible. Every day Moushi would take from the earnings of his butcher shop the amount needed for the day's purchases:

> Dad would tell us, 'Today we need half a liter of cooking oil. Go to Kassem's and get half a pound of sugar. Tomorrow, another half-pound.' It is not like now: ten packets of flour at a time, ten kilos of couscous! If we don't have ten packets of chickpeas in the cupboard, we're not happy, whereas back there, to cook your *t'fina* you had enough with 250 grams of chick peas, and the following week you'd buy more. You only had small expenses every morning.   *(Rosette)*

Everyone remembers the detailed strategies for daily adjustment, but nobody mentions poverty. Except during the war, they were never short of food in Dar-Refayil. No household is said to have been destitute. Descriptions of food purchases, the preparation of meals, and the contents of menus abound, as if the type of life each household led could be defined by how much was eaten at each meal.

Although most food shopping was done daily, some foodstuffs were stocked seasonally or continuously. For Jewish families these were spices, coffee, salt, and summer fruits and vegetables (peppers, olives, tomatoes, oranges, and quinces) preserved for winter use: 'We piled our preserves into jars and used them throughout the winter. We decorated the kitchen with these jars. We'd put in peppers, tomatoes, sugar, fruit preserves, especially for Passover, you had to decorate your jars [with many colours]' (Clarisse). In Muslim families it was the staple semolina that was permanently stocked. Cereals, especially wheat, made up the majority of their diet. The Jews, particularly the Senoussis, who could draw upon Moushi's butcher shop, ate more meat. Cheese was as rare in Jewish as in Muslim households; it was not an important product of Algerian agriculture.

Until the 1950s, domestic amenities were minimal. Then a few gramophones made their appearance with young people like Claude, Charlie, Michel, and Robert, for whom they represented the main part of their meagre teenage entertainment. The appearance of the first car driven by a working man in town in 1958 is narrated as a major event: 'Nobody had a car. Ooh! When a working man bought a car, we'd all turn around to watch. The first to buy a D.S. (a Citroën) was Lucien G. It was the first D.S. in Sétif. When we saw a car go past, it was a major event! We'd normally only see carts – long plank, two wheels, and a horse, that was it!' (Clarisse).

Clothing purchases are another powerful theme in the description of daily economic adjustments. Clothes, like food, serve in narratives as indicators of status in the social hierarchy. In these large families, clothes were passed down from one child to the next, and when all the siblings had worn them out they were given to Muslim families. Thus only the firstborn could enjoy new clothes:

The oldest child's clothes would be passed down to the next one. We'd buy only for the first born, if that was all the family could afford. For example, I always had new clothes, because I was the eldest daughter, and my dresses fitted my next sister. She was about the same size as I. Mom would sew the hems. If one was too short, she'd make it longer by letting down the hem or by adding a strip of cloth.   *(Rosette)*

In material life, the rule in Dar-Refayil was to waste nothing. Clothes increased in use value by circulating among children. Darning sessions following the weekly wash are remembered vividly by women. Once again, the imagery is a narrative metaphor underlining modest people's daily heroism. Luckily, the domestic community had several good seamstresses; a good number of children were dressed by their mothers or their elder sisters:

Parents would often go without for their children. They even didn't buy [clothes for themselves]. We'd go through the winter wearing lace-up shoes. Then, when they were worn out, we'd be told, 'Take the shoes to the cobbler!' Even socks, when they were full of holes, our mother would take a piece of wool of another colour and darn them, and we'd wear them. Since our shoes came up quite high, you couldn't see it. My mother would also do our shirts. Well, the house lady would darn every week: one day of mending, one day of washing, and one day of ironing. Everything had to be mended, even if there was a little hole. We never bought any underwear.

(*Rosette*)

An exception to this rule was made for festivals. Among Jews, the rule was that no expense be spared for religious holidays. Boys did particularly well as a result of this custom, because it was crucial to wear new clothes for the holiday services in the synagogue. There the economic status of each family could be deciphered, and any change in its finances would be judged by the young men's attire. This is how Guy describes these public events:

For all the holidays, you had to have a pair of new shoes or a new suit or a blazer or a new pair of trousers. You had to have something new on. It's amazing; it was symbolic. You needed something new to justify the holiday – well, at least for the important ones; Pesach [Passover], Pentecost,[6] Rosh Hashana, Yom Kippur. So the parents would go out dressed up like royalty, like lords. 'Ah! Look, that's the Senoussi boy, there's the Bakoushe boy, and there's the Akoun boy.' So they [the chatterboxes] would already be interpreting the signs of everybody's financial fortune, the state of each family's finances. They'd look at someone and say 'Ooh! He's got on the same pair of shoes, his father is obviously broke!'

As public events, the holidays were occasions both for community evalua- tion of the positions of the families and for disguising one's status through one's attire. New clothes for holidays were purchased mainly in Jewish- owned stores that gave discounts to their coreligionists for the occasion. These discounts were a kind of financial backing for the community as a whole, allowing it to maintain a high profile in the local multiethnic context at key points in the religious calendar.

Memory recounts this complexity by emphasizing the *practical and incorporated* form of social status as it was inscribed in daily life. It is as if the body had recorded these signs of distinction and acted as a historiog- rapher, a sociologist of the past.

Finding a trade to support oneself

Nothing speaks louder in Dar-Refayil's narrative memory than the anxiety to survive economically and to prepare for working life. Men's memories here are more versatile than women's. Their main recollections of teenage years first focus on the bar mitzvah, described as an initiation into manhood, and then shift to efforts to train for and obtain a job as if this were the logical consequence of becoming a man. Women's narratives most often mention their inventive strategies for managing limited daily budgets. Thus both men's and women's accounts seem preoccupied by the pursuit of material resources and social advancement. From the end of the Second World War onward, the key struggle for Jewish families in Sétif could be summarized as improving their social status and increasing their income. Jewish narratives seem to be more concerned with this socioeconomic struggle than with the threat of war.

Most of Dar-Refayil's residents were manual workers, artisans, employees in small businesses, or the operators of small food stores. The Senoussis were at the top of the occupational hierarchy: Moushi was his own boss, and his butcher shop provided the family significant quantities of meat. Mardochée Akoun was a travelling merchant selling wheat and other grains. After his death in 1942, his eldest son, René, assumed responsibility for the family, working as a hairdresser's assistant and eventually setting up his own salon. Polo Bakoushe had a house-painting business; El-'Ayyashi was what might be called a self-taught dentist, having learned the job while working with a relative; Khlifa, Zakiya's husband, was a baker; Bou-Slimo worked as a waiter, and Sayid, Latifa's husband, sold chickens. Khadidja earned her living as the building's caretaker, a sort of concierge, as they called her. She took care of the housekeeping and made sure that the garbage was collected. Farida's husband was a farmer, but since she disliked country life she lived in town with her two sons. Little Mouna was divorced and raising her four children on her own salary; an assistant seamstress at the military hospital, she was one of the first women to work, out of sheer necessity, outside the domestic and family network.

Indeed, during and after the Second World War, Jewish women worked only if they absolutely had to. Thus Madeleine began to work as an assistant accountant only a few years after her mother's death. Her sister Yvette was first a cashier, then a sales assistant in various businesses. Claire was trained as a nurse and worked for a year or two before the family left for France. Zahra, René Akoun's wife, also had to work after the death of her father-in-law to meet the needs of a large family. She had a job as a nurse's aide at the Sétif hospital. Anna Akoun was a seamstress who worked at home. Most of her customers were Muslim women: she was expert at making traditional Arab dresses.[7] Working at home meant that women could still carry out their domestic duties and that their husbands could continue to control their activities. This tradition prevented many of Dar-Refayil's women from working outside the home. Eldest brothers exercised authority over their sisters' professional destinies, as Clarisse explains: 'I wanted to be a hairdresser, like my brother. He told my mother, "I don't want to see her doing this job. It's bad for the lungs. Even ladies' hairdressing, it's a misery. Don't let her get into that. She'll work with her sister!"' The development of female labor during this period was thus simultaneously an essential part of the struggle for the family's economic survival and an increasing threat to agnatic authority. This process distinguished the fate of Jewish women from that of Muslim women in Dar-Refayil, who were restricted to domestic chores. The strongly patriarchal structures of the Muslim family made it impossible for them to acquire any occupational training or financial autonomy. Farida became an employee of the mayor's household only after her husband's death.

Most of the young workers who entered the job market towards the end of the Second World War were barely educated. Very few Jewish men and women at the time had had any significant professional training. In Dar-Refayil, which was quite representative of the situation of Setifian Jews, most youngsters dropped out of school at fourteen or fifteen. At best they would graduate with an elementary school certificate, a degree considered advanced for the time in such a small town.[8] Secular education was rarely seen as the first step towards social advancement; instead it tended to be seen as an obstacle to the necessary entry into the labour force. Benjamin Senoussi waited impatiently to turn sixteen, the minimum school-leaving age according to French law, to enter the working world. He and his sisters summed up their memories of his school career in an oft-told anecdote:

When he went to school, he'd spend a year on the same lesson – all year. And she [his older sister Yvette] had not realized this. One day, she asked him, 'Benjamin, where are you in your lesson?' 'Well . . . I've got to the page on the boxer.' 'And how long are you going to dwell on the page on the boxer? It's been six years!' *(Rosette)*

Many of these young Jews learned their jobs within the family. Men would carry on in the same trade as their father or work in the same business as an elder brother. When the family business could no longer employ all the adult sons, the eldest would try to persuade an outside employer to give their younger brothers jobs. Women's training and jobs were handed down in the matriline or within the network of female relatives. This is how Anna's daughters both became seamstresses. Clarisse did not continue in the trade, which she disliked; she married before having time to consider another occupation. Her sister got a job as a seamstress in town. The family thus formed an effective network for occupational training, a process that helps explain why low-income families did not encourage their children to pursue public education even though this would eventually have allowed them considerable upward mobility.

Thus Moushi adamantly pursued this strategy, keeping his sons at home and thereby sacrificing their educational and professional progress. After Sarah's death he refused to send Marcel to the *lycée* in Constantine, where he could have acquired an excellent secondary education, claiming that he could not afford to. Marcel therefore went into the meat business at the age of thirteen, taking care of the accounts and the till as his mother had done. Moushi would not let his son work with the meat. It was he who cut up the carcasses and waited on the customers. Marcel was responsible for buying the animals and sending them to the abattoirs for slaughter, and he would hang the sides of meat on the display racks, but he never had the experience of cutting and serving at his father's side. This situation became unbearable when he married Rosette. Eventually, the two of them could no longer put up with their economic dependence on Moushi. Leaving a distraught Moushi behind, they went to Algiers, where a rich Jewish cattle trader was opening a 'modern' butcher shop downtown. Marcel's lack of training had closed to him any alternative but departure. Had he stayed in Sétif he could not have worked for another kosher butcher in town without competing with his own father. The choice for him was between remaining trapped in the family machine or leaving, and he chose the latter in 1950, just after his brother Eddie married Clarisse Akoun.

Eddie had also started off in the meat business with his father, and his career proved similar to that of his elder brother. His marriage and the birth of children forced him to quit his father's business, which was inadequate to the needs of two growing families. In 1953 he found a maintenance job in the Bordj-Bou-Arreridj hospital. Every week the young father would commute between the two towns to spend the sabbath with his family. This tiring arrangement began to involve great risks when the war of independence broke out in 1954 because of the frequent ambushes on the road. The family became so worried about Eddie's future that his elder brother suggested that he join him in Algiers, where he promised that they would do good business in meat together. Eddie and Clarisse eventually left Sétif in 1958.

Charlie took his brother's place in Moushi's shop, but he had to leave for military service in Constantine towards the middle of the fifties. In 1958 he married a Jewish woman in Constantine and settled there, where he worked for the post office.

Claude entered his father's shop when he dropped out of high school at fourteen, but by now times had changed. Moushi's little shop could hardly make ends meet. There were three kosher butchers in Sétif, and competition was stiff. Moushi's customers were mainly working class. He had to keep his prices low, and sold to many of them on credit. It was Claude who had to go out every month and collect the debts. Moushi had refused to modernize the business as Marcel had suggested, but given his clientele this might not have been financially viable in any case. Meat was bought daily and immediately sold, since there was no means of refrigeration. Jewish housewives in Sétif were unfamiliar with steaks and other grilled cuts. Stew meat was the typical purchase, as Claude recalls:

In Sétif, my father sold meat on the bone. He belonged to the old school: he never took the meat off the bone, so there was no roast beef or steak. People would 'cook' a lot [overcook]. They wouldn't grill their meat as we do today, except for liver [and gizzards] and lamb cutlets. They would only cook stews and simmered dishes. At home, though my father was a butcher, we didn't eat beef steaks. My mother would cook stews every day. My father would carve up meat on the bone. We'd call it the 'American cut'. We'd cut into the meat with a saw. This is the way it had been done for thousands of years. It had more flavor, the bone would give it flavor, but the presentation was different.

By this time the butcher shop was open only part-time, being located in the covered market, which was closed in the afternoons. Eventually Moushi became weary of this declining business. In the year before his death he was holding onto it only to gather the money necessary for the bar mitzvah of his youngest son Benjamin. Without telling anyone but Claude, he considered selling the business, and in 1959 he went into partnership with a Muslim butcher. When he fell ill and died in 1960, he was 'fed up', says Claude. 'He didn't want to work any longer. His nerves were worn out.'

Claude was left without a job and without any training. For a few months after his father's death, he took on several small jobs in various businesses, including that of salesman in a shoe store. But he was quite naturally drawn to work in the meat trade. His brothers Marcel and Eddie encouraged him to join them in Algiers, where they were doing very well. On his deathbed, Moushi had charged Marcel with the responsibility of looking after his younger brothers as tradition required him to do. The family's departure for Algiers in 1961 was a tremendous relief to Claude:

I was certainly very pleased to leave Dar-Refayil – not because I didn't like the house or my home town; I was pleased because I couldn't see any job openings for me there. If it hadn't been for the war, I would have stayed in Algiers, and I would have done well there. It was bigger, and there were more possibilities, unlike in

Sétif . . . Anyway, a lot of people from Sétif were leaving, even before the war, just as teenagers, because they couldn't find a job. They went to Paris, all over the place. Marcel left because he couldn't stay with my father. My father's business was too small and couldn't give him large amounts of money. My father never told him to go away, but he wanted to make it on his own. So I was really pleased to go to Algiers, because since Marcel and Eddie had two shops, I hoped that one of them would be able to teach me the meat trade – that I was going to make a start, to take off. I was a bit lost, but I was happy to be learning a trade I really liked and that I still like today. Even when I was a kid, I wanted to move on, to have a trade so I could get on in the world.

Claude's logic makes it clear: the real war in which the young Jews of the fifties were engaged was not so much the war of independence as the struggle to find a job – a trade to help them defend themselves in the pursuit of social and economic advancement. Yet in contrast to other Jews of their generation these youngsters from a small traditional town did not see the pursuit of higher education as a way of achieving these aims. More pressing and immediate was the need to feed large families living on meagre incomes. In addition, as we have seen, many young Jews schooled before the Second World War had been excluded from French schools in 1942. Hounded by economic necessity, they did not return to school after the war, but they never lost their passionate desire to climb the social ladder and become fully integrated into the French society of which they had been legally a part since the end of the nineteenth century. To get on as Jews meant being economically autonomous and achieving the same level as Frenchmen if not a higher one. This perspective was not shared by the Muslims of Dar-Refayil, whose immediate aim was to end the shame of colonization, of which they foresaw the downfall towards the end of the fifties.

Remembering women's lives

In the context of the house's stories, women's memories fall within the framework of dual-gender, multireligious collective memory, but when they talk about their particular place in a complex social system they re-create their lives as opposed to or distinct from those of men. The collective interviews I undertook when the women were gathered to prepare for Passover generated *gendered* memories, and I often asked myself whether I had not provoked this process myself by my unplanned feminist solidarity. One of the striking findings of this interviewing process was that women sought to monopolize the house's collective memory – to seize symbolic power, through verbal skill, to make up for the fragile position of women in the past domestic community. It was as if they were getting even with history by recapturing power in words, 'creatively deforming their [past] submission' (Herzfeld 1991b:81). In many instances, I felt that Dar-Refayil's story was *their* story, the story of *their* lives, *their* courage, *their* heroism.

The house's memories are dominated by women's recollections, discourse, and vision. Yet there are some ambiguities in this gendered formulation of the domestic epic. Women speak about a universe in which they want their presence to be central; they spent most of their time there and were responsible for the most necessary and repetitive tasks. At the same time, they constantly bemoan their imprisonment in a world which stifled their aspirations for career and personal autonomy. When women insist that, although the custom and the authority were on the masculine side, in practice it was they who exercised real power in the daily domestic routine, their memories in fact aim at symbolically reversing the past rule and ideology of patriarchy.[9] Women's memories of their past status and experience oscillate between two poles: submissive in the domain of symbolic and legitimate authority, dominant in the practical exercise of domestic life.[10]

Jewish women often describe Muslim families as fortresses in which women lived cloistered under male control and lacked access to secular education. Their narratives aim to distance themselves from this. Contrasting their own destinies with those of Muslim women is a process of identity that combines gender and ethnic-religious dimensions. The leitmotif 'We didn't live like Arab women, we were more advanced!' has obvious historical meaning: it is more significant in the narratives of Jewish women born after the First World War. The period in which they reached adulthood and entered the labour market was also a transitional period in which the traditional structures of the patriarchal and patrilineal Jewish family were being seriously called into question. These changes in family relationships and authority structure were not simply the result of female pressure; men had to turn their backs on the agnatic system and on patrilineal trades if they wanted to improve their socioeconomic status. The post-First World War generation thus prepared the ground for those to come.

These developments had more effect on women whose mothers had experienced traditions similar to those imposed on Muslim women. Women like Sarah, born at the turn of the century, had only been able to choose between obedience and escape into death or the fringes of society. Thus Alice, Rosette's mother, describes her marriage as a teenager as a transaction between relatives in which she had had no say. She had been adopted as a young girl by a maternal aunt.[11] The only child of her adoptive family, unlike many young girls of her age, she had been raised in material comfort. Her adoptive father was a widely respected civil servant. One of her first cousins, over ten years older than she, had asked for her hand when she was only sixteen and quite incapable of understanding what was happening to her:

I was raised by wealthy people, an uncle and an aunt who hadn't had any children of their own. One day, this aunt came to Sétif – I must still have been very little because soon after this they put me straight into nursery school. My aunt said to her sister, who was my mother, 'You have so many children. Your house is swarming with them!' (She spoke in Arabic, you see.) And then she said, 'Give me one of your daughters. I'll raise her, I'll look after her. At least she can keep me company, since I can't have any children. See that one? She's got lovely blue eyes. Give me that one!' And she wrapped me in a rag, with some linen, some underwear, petticoats like in the old days. She put me with all that in a *sarwel* [baggy trousers], and they took me away like that, tucked under their arm, to Bougie. And there, they were the ones who married me off – who arranged my betrothal and did everything that had to be done. I grew up with them; they gave me a beautiful trousseau. And it was in Bougie that I met my husband, who was my cousin[12] and whom I'd never met before. He was ten years older than me. He was a womanizer; he had mistresses all over the place. Another cousin of mine, Léon, knew him very well; they were good friends. He said to him, 'So, aren't you going to get married? Come and see all these young girls at the wedding [of one of my female cousins].' All the girls were sitting down. I was sixteen. We were playing jacks on the floor. And I saw these two cousins come up and stand there looking at us. So he told him, 'Go on, choose. I swear I'll arrange it all for you.' He [the future husband] said, 'That little plump one there. I like her, who's she?'

At this point, Rosette commented on the narrative: 'Like in the old days, the Arabs – *The Arabian Nights*.' Alice went on:

Then the other cousin said, 'That one, *hede romiya*, she's a Catholic, she's been invited by the family. Careful, hands off!', just to see how he would react. And he answered, 'Really, I swear, I like the look of her. She's got lovely eyes, she's beautiful, she's got pale skin.' . . . So the other told him, 'What are your intentions towards her, then?' 'I swear, if she's Jewish, I'll make a move. I'll tell my mother to ask for her hand tonight.' See, his mother was praying every day for him to marry a Jewish girl, because he was always going around with Catholic women. So he told his mother, 'Well, this is it. I've found a shoe to fit me. It's the little Alice who lives with her aunt in Bougie.' So she said, 'Ah! That one, she's young. She still sucks her thumb, she's at school.' But in the end she came [to our house] and said, 'Well, I've come to ask you something, and if you turn me down, I don't know what will happen.' She meant trances, the *djnun* [evil spirits], that she'd spit fire. So my cousin Léon told me, 'You see this gentleman? Give him a kiss; he's your cousin' – without telling me that he had asked for my hand in marriage. I was still like this, looking down.

Alice's narrative unfolds around a theme presented as the defining principle of her destiny as an early twentieth-century young North African Jewish woman: a woman dispossessed of her free will, her life orchestrated by others. She describes her whole life as a succession of 'deals' contracted against her will by 'strangers'. She was raised by people she had never met, who became her parents. She was married to a man she had never met, who became her husband. Her narrative is structured as a fairy tale. Some women of Alice's generation almost never left their houses even to go to the marketplace for daily shopping. Gilda would ask her son Claude to go to the grocery store every afternoon on his way home from school.

It was only during the interwar period that women began to acquire some autonomy. In part because of the economic pressures on families, the fate of young women came to be decided not just by their fathers and elder brothers but by economic necessity. Rosette, born in the early twenties, claims to represent this generation of rebellious women who had decided to take control over their lives and to do away with the injustices their mothers had suffered. Rosette certainly played a decisive role in Marcel's distancing himself from paternal control, but her sisters-in-law and female cousins in Dar-Refayil often remained under the authority of their male relatives until they had been 'married off'. Liliane, Guy Bakoushe's elder sister, had to give up the idea of pursuing her studies after the age of seventeen because her father thought it would be better for her to get married as soon as possible.

Unmarried women stayed at home, whereas sons were encouraged to spend most of their time out in the street. Women's diversions outside the house were usually chaperoned; at local dance parties brothers watched over their sisters, and sometimes discouraged would-be suitors. Brothers showed more zeal in controlling their sisters than did their fathers. Thus Eddie said that Moushi only rarely made comments to his daughters about their outings: '*We* were the ones who jealously guarded our sisters, not he. He'd say, 'Go look after your sister.' So if we'd see her talk to a young man, we'd say, 'Why did you talk to him?'' Always chaperoned by their brothers when away from home, young women made up their own private domestic leisure activities, which were no less convivial. Rosette explains:

If one of us was being punished, no one would go [to the movies]. We'd stay in and have fun together. In the evening, none of us would go out, not ever! On Saturdays we'd hold young women's gatherings; it was *the young women's house* [my emphasis], and the young men were sitting at the cafés, *they* were allowed to do that. But young women, we'd get together in a room, we'd eat sweets and chat. We didn't have much to talk about, since we all led pretty much the same life, and we had no secrets, either, because we were so carefully guarded.

Dar-Refayil's young women in the forties had much the same level of education as their brothers. They all abandoned their schooling around the age of sixteen to enter the work world in an attempt to supplement their families' incomes. Girls' education was different from boys' only in that they received no religious instruction. With their entirely secular training, women were better suited than their brothers to entry into the non-familial labour market. Thus, towards the end of the fifties, Yvette took her first job when her younger brothers and sisters were still at school and Moushi's business was on the verge of collapse. Other women, such as Clarisse, worked only for a short time between leaving school and getting married. Yet during this brief period of relative economic autonomy the girls began to go to the movies on the weekends without their brothers. Clarisse and Yvette sometimes even dared to stay out after the movie and go for a walk along the Rue de Constantine, where they would wave distant greetings to their male friends sitting on the terraces of the cafés. From time to time they would even go so far as to sit down and enjoy a pastry. For women like Yvette and Clarisse the fifties were years of a freedom timidly but tenaciously grasped. Real independence for women in their leisure activities came as they acquired financial autonomy and started to contribute to the family budget. For many of them, though, this period was a brief break between teenage years supervised by their elder brothers and married life under the relatively strict control of their in-laws.

Since women's leisure activities were limited to outings with neighbours or brothers, most Jewish marriages in Dar-Refayil until the fifties were contracted within a relatively limited social network. Consanguinal marriage had been very common in the previous generation. Marriages among neighbours often ended in marriage among kinsmen such as those in Dar-Refayil since the thirties. Thus Anna married off three of her children to close neighbours, the children of Nonna Ayashe, Moushi's maternal aunt. Until the forties, Nonna's family lived in two rooms on the upper floor, opposite the house's gate and almost next door to the Akouns' lodgings. René married Zahra Ayashe in 1936; a few years later his brother Raymond married Germaine Ayashe and in 1948, after the Ayashes had left the house and given their rooms to relatives of the Akouns, Anna's eldest daughter Odette married Nonna's son, George. This chain of marriages between neighbouring groups of siblings continued in 1950 when Eddie Senoussi, himself related to the Ayashes, married Clarisse Akoun,

Anna's youngest daughter. This marriage was the latest version of what everyone in Dar-Refayil viewed as a matrimonial model, 'marrying your neighbour'.

This model inspired many jokes and even an Arabic song composed collectively in Dar-Refayil that Eddie's friends would sing to tease him. Eddie and Clarisse's marriage was the culmination of a long history of teenagers' socializing in the house which was encouraged by parents as soon as children reached the age of puberty. Thus what looks like a series of arrangements between Nonna Ayashe and Anna Akoun, two widows heading large families, and then between Anna and Moushi Senoussi was in fact the product of a long-term matrimonial strategy that consisted in keeping sons within the agnatic group and controlling its women. The story of Eddie and Clarisse's marriage presents it as the successful implementation of the notion of religious, family, and domestic endogamy.

It was said that Eddie did not wear himself out looking for a bride: he only had to walk across the balcony. So Clarisse married the man with whom she had shared most of her teenage pastimes. As an adolescent, she had often gone out with her brother Louis and with Yvette and Eddie Senoussi. She told her marriage story as the happy outcome of the ongoing attempt to preserve family cohesion. Her narrative is typically feminine in underlining the theme of stability: getting married meant putting down roots in the domestic and family sphere. In several instances it recalls the story of Alice, with its central theme of female disempowerment:

My [would-be] father-in-law came to see my mother and told her, 'Well, I've come to ask for Clarisse's hand.' I wasn't there at the time. When I came home that night, she told me, 'Moushi was here today asking for your hand. So what do you want to do?' I said, 'I want to get married.' And that's how we got engaged, and we were married a year later. We used to see each other before [the wedding]. No, we didn't do like Arabs; Moushi knew about it, and Yvette too. So I crossed the balcony. We went out of this door, and then I came in through that door [opposite]. And Eddie carried me up the stairs to the the balcony [owners']. So I never left the house. My in-laws were very kind to me. I knew them well, they liked me, and I always liked them and respected them, too. After my wedding, I could still see my brothers and sisters all day. Every morning, I went home, and my mother was there. So for me, nothing much had changed!

Women describe their marriages as if they were their major asset. Their reconstructions show that marriage is simultaneously the beginning of a long journey and the fulfillment of one's personal destiny (see Valensi and Wachtel 1991). Women remembered the tiniest details of their weddings and the negotiations and transactions that preceded them. By contrast, men knew very little about these details and seemed unwilling to recall them as they did those of their bar mitzvahs. Marriage was a female matter and represented the female condition of their time.

At the core of these narratives is the dominant theme of women's lack of control over their lives. In matrimonial policy and negotiations, family strategies overruled the bride's wishes. Even though family strategies were often imposed on both sons and daughters, it was women who constituted themselves as the prime concern of the marriage process, and it was their vulnerability that marriage underscored. Their narratives transformed women into the central characters of the matrimonial system and the heroines of its festivities. Madeleine was presented as the only woman in Dar-Refayil to have 'married for love'. In 1945 she married Joseph, her second cousin, who had come to Sétif from Algiers during the war with a message for Moushi from his father. It was 'love at first sight', the women say. Yet Madeleine had also married a consanguinal relative, a preferred marriage in this traditional Jewish community.

One of the narrative devices displaying the theme of female disempowerment is age at marriage. Alice was married at sixteen, and her daughter Rosette was only eighteen when she was married to Marcel. Clarisse was about the same age when she married Eddie. Although women's condition had changed slightly between Alice's and Rosette's generation, their age at marriage had not changed much: Jewish families still made an effort to marry off their daughters in their mid-teens. The emphasis on brides' ages in women's memories allows narrators to underline the weakness of their position in matrimonial negotiations – their being 'merchandised' without regard for their own wishes. This is how Rosette told the story of her marriage to Marcel. Years later, she often complained to her mother about the unhappy marriage that Alice had arranged for her:

How did *I* meet my husband? I was very young, sixteen or seventeen. I knew nothing about life or anything else. At Charlie's communion,[13] I didn't know the [Senoussi] family. Gilda is my mother's sister, so on the sabbath I went to the communion. I said to Mom, 'But I don't know anyone!' She said, '*Meqsofa* [impudent girl]! You'll go to your aunt's; I can't go myself.' And at this communion, Madeleine was just married, I think. She ululated and said, 'Ooh! This girl, how pretty she is! She'd be good for Marcel.' Now, I was only a kid; I didn't know her. She took me by the hand and told me, 'Well, starting today, you're my brother's fiancée' – and this when I still liked to skip and play hopscotch. And two weeks after this communion, Moushi sent a message to my mother: 'Can I come and visit you with Gilda so that we can ask for your daughter's hand?' She answered, 'She's still very young!' He said, 'Exactly. Protect her, *ester'ha*, so that she won't grow up and find out about wicked things.' That was it; as soon as we grew up, girls had to be married off. And this when I was still playing hopscotch and skipping games with Julie Z.

Women's accounts of marriage are ambiguous. They heroize brides while at the same time emphasizing the constraints imposed on them. When they describe these important events of their personal lives, women are in fact producing a discourse on the dilemmas of the agnatic system, the failures of the family logic, and the challenges faced by the Jews of Sétif within these structures. Their memories present marriage as central to the social fate of Sétif's Jews and place women at the heart of this process. Rosette's narrative is a good illustration of this symbolic procedure. It is quite different from that of Clarisse, who married a familiar man. The two sisters-in-law, who did not really have the opportunity to live together in Dar-Refayil (Eddie and Clarisse having lived there after Rosette and Marcel had left for Algiers), have different relationships to marriage. Rosette associates all her experiences prior to her departure for Algiers with the representation of an archaic society in which women were stifled and dependent. For her, marriage was a key point in this structure oppressing women. As for Clarisse, she did not have to leave her family when she married Eddie. She could see her mother and siblings every day by simply walking across the balcony, and her in-laws were also familiar faces, both neighbours and distant 'cousins' of her parents. Nor was there any real social difference between the Senoussis and the Akouns. By contrast, Rosette claims to have come from a better-off family which had suddenly undergone financial reverses when her father died a few years before her marriage. Thus she lacked the financial means to aspire to anything but marriage into a low-income family. Her description of her house before marriage underlines this social difference from the Senoussis:

Our apartment was on a two-apartment floor, and *we'd close it* [my emphasis].[14] Each apartment had six or seven rooms, three kitchens, a gate downstairs, always closed . . . a real bourgeois house with a beautiful white marble staircase. It was located opposite to the Haudurau Company, a pasta and semolina factory. We had always lived in this house, since my great-grandparents' time.

Rosette experienced her marriage and her move to Dar-Refayil as the social regression that sealed a hypogamous union. Her life as a married woman in her father-in-law's house was marred by clashes with Moushi and in particular with Gilda, even though the latter was her maternal aunt. Rosette's account of her marriage underlines a major dimension of the matrimonial process in Dar-Refayil: the endogamy practised in the house was above all socioeconomic. Until recently, marriage in Sétif entailed a dowry that was reused later on as the dowry of the groom's sister. Thus, especially (if not exclusively) among upper-class families (see Glazer 1982), dowries constituted mobile capital circulating through the community. In lower-income families (the great majority in Sétif), a dowry was not required since many potential brides had none. Only a trousseau, which the girls themselves had spent their adolescence embroidering, would be provided.[15] So Rosette, like other Jewish girls in Dar-Refayil, had no dowry. Her resentment over her marriage speaks to the socioeconomic reversal her family had had to endure after her father's death. It also underlines the major rationale for domestic endogamy in Dar-Refayil: these marriages inside the house excluded possible conjugal conflicts generated by socioeconomic differences between the spouses' families.

Another form of female subjugation through conjugal duties and the marriage structure, motherhood, was imperative for brides to be recognized as full-fledged members of their husbands' patriline. Clarisse amply fulfilled this major duty. Rosette's was a different experience altogether. As a mother-in-law rather than a maternal aunt, Gilda daily reminded Rosette of her various spousal obligations. She frequently blamed Rosette for pushing Marcel to leave the house and his father's business. During one of these arguments, an angry Gilda said that she wished Rosette would never have children or happiness in her marriage. The mother-in-law's wish came true. Rosette never gave offspring to the Senoussi family, and as the elder brother's wife she silently endured the daily harshness of the status of the sterile woman.

Many of these Jewish women in Sétif experienced the maternal obligation through the agony of repeated miscarriages, with the tensions this would cause in their relationships with their husbands and in-laws. Two of Gilda's seven pregnancies ended in miscarriage. Zahra lost two infants and also had two miscarriages. Little Mouna had twins who died at birth when she was twenty. In the following generation, the thought of pregnancy and childbirth often terrified brides, who had seen their mothers' suffering. After the birth of her first child, Clarisse, who was only twenty, became seriously ill. It was first thought that she had scabies, which was prevalent in Sétif at the time. Her rationale conflicts with this explanation, interpreting her discomfort as the psychosomatic syndrome of 'the fear of giving birth', as an Arab physician and a family friend had suggested: 'I was frightened of childbirth. I was young, I didn't realize. I was in such a pain when I gave birth that I thought it was the end. A few hours later I began to develop an internal hemorrhage. I don't know whether it was because I was frightened, but I got spots, like scabies.'

The discovery of sexuality geared entirely towards reproduction is also remembered as a violent physical experience for these teenage brides, who had been told time and again that sex was horror:

On my wedding night, we went to sleep at the Hôtel de France. As long as there were people around, I wasn't frightened. But as soon as I found myself alone with my husband – I got the jitters when we entered the hotel, which was something well-brought up young women would never do. So we went up to our room, I can't remember the number . . . and he unbuttons my dress. I was terrified! He was unbuttoning my dress! I told him, 'Take me back to my mother, I don't want to stay with you. I want to go to my mother's house!' 'I understand how you feel,' he said, 'but you're my wife now.'   *(Rosette)*

Women's accounts of their matrimonial experience have the look of a marathon. Marriage begins on a positive note as the culmination of family cohesiveness, but it soon develops into a fierce struggle with fate and family constraints. After the crusade for motherhood comes the responsibility of running a low-income household. As part of this effort the young wives of the fifties took jobs in town in addition to the washing, the mending, and the shopping. In Dar-Refayil, married women were practically and emotionally assisted in these duties by the solidarity of the female community. In women's memories, the complex network of female assistance makes up for the harshness of their domestic responsibilities. This system saved Little Mouna when she decided to divorce her violent husband towards the end of the forties. The event ended up being a tragedy for this young woman, who had received no training and raised four children on her own:

It was the neighbours who helped me. I had never worked in my life. And Anna told me, 'My girl, it's the only way out for you, you'll have to find a job.' There was solidarity in the house, that's why we stayed so close to each other. You see, when I talk about them [the neighbours], they're like my family. So I didn't even have a dress [to go to work]. My dress was all torn. I had to hold it like this, with a safety pin, to cover me up, because I couldn't afford to buy a dress.   *(Little Mouna)*

By underlining the harshness of women's lives, my hosts were demonstrating that they had been brave before my time: 'Look here, you with your degrees from a French university, see how we, your elder sisters, struggled silently every day just to survive.' Their strategies of social and personal survival were solidarity, complicity, and conviviality. Echoing accounts of hardship are peaceful images of communal comfort:

After lunch, we'd go down to have coffee with Little Mouna. My mother would go down to take her afternoon nap there, because it felt good. As soon as she came in, she'd get onto the bed. You see, we were easy with each other, we'd feel at home everywhere. She [Little Mouna] would call, 'Come down, come and have a cup of coffee!' We'd sit on the floor and sip our coffee, and then I'd go back to work.

(Clarisse)

Female conviviality sometimes overcame religious distinctions. Jewish and Muslim women occasionally spent time together as they performed their various chores in the courtyard. On some evenings Gilda would stay downstairs chatting with her Muslim neighbours until she'd fall asleep on her stool.

Neighbours as friends

Memory uses three major criteria for classifying individuals in the house: gender, age, and religion. The two latter are particularly emphasized in accounts of adolescence, a passage in the life cycle which stimulates the discovery of boundaries of various kinds. In Dar-Refayil there were no personal affinities between Jewish and Muslim adolescents. Adolescence split their paths apart, and thus youngsters' socializing followed strict ethnic lines. Similarly, they made friends with teenagers of the exact same age because, as Elie Akoun explained, two years made a great difference when you were a teenager. Finally, given the difference between the lives of men and women, very few friendships developed across the gender barrier.

Among adults, as we have seen, similar distinctions existed. All the accounts mention the archetypical friendship between Moushi and Polo Bakoushe. Though they were not exactly the same age, they were virtually the only living Jewish fathers in the domestic community. Their sons carried on these strong ties. Claude Senoussi and Guy Bakoushe had been inseparable since their early days despite differences in personality. Today, Claude lives in Marseilles and Guy in a Parisian suburb but their friendship survives as the house of childhood appears in their memories as a symbolic link:

I used to see Claude a lot. I think it was because there had been such a strong friendship between his father and mine. And then Gilda was very kind. I remember when we were kids, she'd put both of us on her lap, Claude and me. And you know Claude had had vision problems for quite a while. In the beginning, no one would believe him except me, maybe because my friendship *blinded* me [my emphasis] because I loved him so much. For me Claude was a brother. When he came to my home, he'd eat at my table, from the same plate. We'd sleep in the same bed. We'd buy the same clothes.   *(Guy)*

Friendships in Dar-Refayil developed out of necessity and in the course of shared activities rather than from mere personal affinity. Among Jewish adolescent boys, the period preceding the bar mitzvah encouraged peer socializing, as with the famous trio made up of Elie Akoun, Charlie Senoussi, and Robert Akoun, Little Mouna's son.

A similar practical chemistry forged the link between Clarisse and Yvette, who are sisters-in-law now because they were friends then. Their outings to the movies on weekends often recur in their narratives as emblems of their then-claimed independence and resourcefulness. Here again female friendship is displayed as a weapon in their struggle for autonomy. Yvette showed the most aptitude for persuading their parents to let them go out together. At the Senoussis', Saturday afternoon was devoted to the weekly ritual of distributing pocket money to the children. Boys and girls of the same age were given the same amount. The youngest had only enough to buy sweets, but some children would persuade others to pool their meagre funds and manage to get some benefit out of the others' shares. Thus Benjamin would exploit his younger sister's naïvety extorting her pittance by promising to buy sweets for them both, saving his own funds for other investments. Yvette would manage to add to her share of the weekly allowance the profits she had snatched 'from the bottom of the shopping basket': when she wanted to fit in one or two extra visits to the cinema in the middle of the week, she would make sure that she was the one to do the food shopping and would inflate the prices of the groceries purchased.

The links forged within the house structured the diversions outside. The young people's accounts of their leisure activities are still family and house stories. When they went dancing, the girls were chaperoned by their brothers or their closest neighbours. This is how Yvette and Clarisse met their husbands. The two friends would go out with Eddie, Louis (Clarisse's brother), and Jeannot, Eddie's best friend, who married Yvette in 1956. The youngsters were carrying the domestic family-oriented world out into the wider one. When they could not afford outings they would organize spontaneous home leisure activities, chatting on the balcony or listening to their elders' tales of the old days. From time to time, improvised dancing parties would take place on the upper terrace.

Remembered life in Dar-Refayil is not entirely made up of hard work and dearth. Recollections subtly render this balance between harsh living conditions and human conviviality, and laughter overlies descriptions of pain. Women excel in the narrative art of balancing happiness and pain – a strategy for moralizing the past human context and humanizing a difficult material world. Laughter has the effect of distancing past hardships and magnifying their present happy results.

The intimacy of distinction: Jews and Muslims living together
The symbolic design of the remembered house thus traces the limits of kinship as it was then understood. Some neighbours were incorporated into the kin group and often addressed as 'cousins'. The term 'neighbours' denoted practical proximity and symbolic distinction; Jewish and Muslim residents viewed each other as 'neighbours'. As Sa'adiya put it, 'In Dar-Refayil there were *us and them* [my emphasis], that's all.' Most descriptions of the house's daily life reflect this distinction, which organizes the remembrance of both material and social structures. For example, it is announced at the outset, as a general overview of the house's design, that the upper floor occupied by Jews was somehow superior in comfort to the lower, Muslim-dominated floor. Memory here uses a material metaphor that highlights the social differences, however minor, within the domestic community. The message could be summarized as: 'We were distinct, but we were alike because we were all in the same boat.' This is echoed in Bou-Slimo's assertion: 'In Dar-Refayil, we lived from day to day, without counting the time. Arabs and Jews, it's all the same! Jews are like us. And anyway we were all the same class, *the lower class, the poor, the wretched* [my emphasis]!' All voices echo Bou-Slimo's, stressing the harmony of the domestic relationships between Jews and Muslims in Dar-Refayil. They remember only what 'good neighbours' they were. Challenging the current media reports of Jewish–Muslim antagonism, Dar-Refayil's collective memoirs emphasize the coresidence 'without animosity' that ruled domestic interactions between Jews and Muslims even in the most critical moments of the war of independence.

I was often surprised by this insistence on presenting interethnic relations as cordial and friendly and wondered whether it was not just another aspect of the heroizing effect inscribed in memory or, perhaps, particularly on the Muslim side, a matter of my hosts' telling me what they thought I wanted to hear. After all, they had invited me to visit them in Sétif, and their descriptions of former harmony were part of the honour I was offered as a guest. As a listener, I was no more neutral: I represented the other side of the former distinction. I was in fact recording remembered past emotions that might have faded with time and with current preoccupations. But if this were the case, how could I explain the spontaneously warm welcome of Dar-Refayil's women when I visited the house in 1980 and the touching invitation that followed? On both Jewish and Muslim sides remembrance was bolstered by a host of practical details.

What, then, is the narrative meaning of the 'harmony' pattern? Women mention it in talking about the practical aspects of daily life in the house, and men refer to it to support their accounts of war and of the town's colonial history. The two structures are in fact the two sides of a narrative contrast: Jewish–Muslim harmony is opposed to the hostility between Christians and both Jews and Muslims. In addition, a contrast is made between the necessary harmony of domestic life and the violent conflicts occurring outside.

On both sides, the memory of claimed accord is a strategy for rationalizing the historical antagonisms that shook colonial Algerian society. On the Muslim side, narratives made much of socioeconomic similarities, erasing any slight difference in status. On both sides, though, remembrance underlined cultural and linguistic affinities as the cement of the multireligious community. Jews and Muslims in Sétif spoke the same language and had similar traditional dress codes and folk beliefs. They liked the same kind of music and enjoyed it together during shared celebrations. Most of all, it was the shared domestic space and the practical necessities of daily life that brought people together who in the political and ideological arena would have been in violent confrontation. Memories of these practical experiences are structurally linked to what produced the harmony between the two religious groups – the practise of everyday life as the social space for resistance to the dehumanizing effects of war (de Certeau 1984). Jews remember the many instances in which their Muslim coresidents protected them from potential outside threats. Once again, it is a female figure that is the archetype of interreligious solidarity:

Until all the neighbours were back home, Farida sat in the courtyard waiting for them. She wasn't the concierge, but sometimes kids would go out for a walk after supper, like my brother Louis and others, and as long as they were out she wouldn't leave her spot by the gate. When they were all back, she'd lock the gate and go to bed. She could have not cared a damn for her neighbours, especially the Jews, but not her! She'd even tell my mother, 'Go on, go to bed. I'll wait for them, don't worry!' These stories about rape [of Jewish women by Arabs], that's all made up by the French, and that's what sparked everything off. The 'natives' got on better with the Jews than with the Christians. And we lived better alongside them.   *(Clarisse)*

Elaborating on the theme of inner harmony is the recurrent expression among Jews: 'We were allowed into their houses.' Children are remembered as the link between Jewish and Muslim families and between women in particular. It was Little Mouna who knitted the layette for Amina, Bou-Slimo and Sa'adiya's first daughter – an indelible image of female cooperation in child raising. Children are remembered as playing in the courtyard regardless of their religion. Now adults, they remember this domestic cooperation by mentioning the sensory dimension of domestic interactions, the odour of baking bread, the odour of cooking, and the small favours women exchanged every day. It was children who brought the missing egg or the half pound of butter forgotten in the previous day's shopping.

The closeness of the two religious groups developed mainly within the framework of the daily chores of domestic life. Exchanges between women were at their peak during the preparations for holidays. When interviewed in 1980, twenty years after the Jews' departure, Muslim women were able to reconstruct Jewish religious festivals, especially their gastronomic aspects, in detail. Sa'adiya remembered how on the sabbath Jewish women would ask her to light the fire under their saucepans or to heat up milk for their children. Jewish and Muslim women had set up a network of mutual obligations and reciprocal ritual prestations: Jewish women would give some of their ritual pastries and other dishes to their Muslim neighbours, who would reciprocate during their own religious festivals. Muslim men were regularly invited to attend the Jewish festivals of the life cycle, mainly weddings and bar mitzvahs. Ritual exchanges were part of the inter-religious code of honour. Memory presents them as the boundary-keepers of the multiethnic order within the domestic community.

Emphasis on Jewish–Muslim harmony in the house does not mean that the distinction between these groups has been forgotten. This was harmony but not anarchic mingling; distinction without hostility. The boundaries between Jewish and Muslim residents were subtly inscribed in the necessary movements of everyday life, the places where these occurred, and the content of interactions. Jewish memories are eager to emphasize these differences, using a wealth of detail that reflects the narrators' drive to put behind them some of their indigenous Maghrebian traits and embrace Western modernity. In particular, they insist that Jewish and Muslim teenagers did not spend time together outside the house and that although Jews entered Muslim households, they never ate there because their dietary laws forbade it.[16] Above all, no intermarriage was ever thought of between Jews and Muslims: religious endogamy was total in the house as in most families of both faiths in Algeria.

Among the negative memories of the close Other are Muslims' memories of a few rich local Jews – a handful of colonists and physicians associated with the colonial power by their social status. Muslims also mention the linguistic differences that began to distance them from their Jewish neighbours and were specifically inscribed in the adoption by Jews of the French naming system. The Jews mention the minor and tacit dissension that appeared at the height of the war of independence, but above all they invoke the social and cultural characteristics of their Muslim neighbours that kept them from sharing their historical aspirations. Women's narratives display a special versatility when they talk about the highly patriarchal Muslim family and the denial of education to Muslim women. For them this represents a historical pattern radically opposed to the one for which Jewish women were striving at the time.

Dar-Refayil's collective memoirs distinguish Jews from Muslims through their religious ascriptions and political aspirations rather than through involvement in the Middle Eastern Arab–Israeli conflict: 'For me, political events were increasingly important [in the 1950s]. They [the Arabs] were on the FLN [Front de Libération Nationale] side, their heritage. And we were on the French side, because we saw ourselves as French' (Guy). In fact, Algerian Jews never adopted more than a neutral position in the colonial conflict (Ayoun and Cohen 1982). Yet their irreversible decision to emigrate to France made their position ambiguous, often being seen by Muslims as a kind of support of the oppressive colonial power. The latter, however, never viewed the Jews as 'real' Europeans. Bou-Slimo's remembrance of Jewish colonists speaks to an aberration rather than a clear political alliance.

The harmony so persistently emphasized in narratives began to be eroded by the 'events' (*les événements*, the folk term for the war of independence), even though the Jewish women emotionally remember the tears of their Muslim neighbours on the day of their departure. The motif of harmony in narratives significantly contrasts with the rather contemptuous and sometimes hostile tone that characterizes the Jewish accounts involving today's Arabs. Hostility emerges in narratives when the phrase 'Arabs' becomes a *generic* category, one that embodies ultimate Otherness. By contrast, harmony is the pattern when relating to the individual and close Arabs of the past. The past spatial closeness is equated with harmony; the current distance and estrangement with hostility. Jewish nostalgia for past harmony evolves as a form of narrative resistance to contemporary anonymous hostility:

Our neighbours were good people. It's the people we didn't know who were mean. And anyway, Arabs were always treacherous. We were often told the story of an Arab woman who had lived with a [Jewish] family in Constantine for almost twenty years. She had raised their children, and the day of the riots, well, she killed the entire family. And this affected us tremendously. But *our* neighbours were very kind. We didn't have anything to resent them for. The day we left, the dentist came up and said to my mother, '*Ma tro'hsh!*' [Don't go!]. So she said to him, 'We're not afraid of you, we trust you, but we're afraid of strangers who might harm our children – the strangers, those of the *douwar* [the countryside].' Even urban Arabs were frightened of them, they really were savages!   *(Clarisse)*

There are different kinds of Arabs. When we say 'the Arabs', I feel hatred, but those are Middle Eastern Arabs. I am not talking about the Arabs who live here [in France], because they don't do us any harm. They work, they earn their living, they have children and families like us, *à la française*. That's fine. If we could live together and get on well as we used to back there, it would be perfect. But the problem in Israel is still not solved. So since I've known the Israeli problem, I am anti-Arab, but not against the Arabs of France. Take Sherif – I have a lot of respect for him. When his wife gave birth, I took her to the hospital in the middle of the night.   *(Rosette)*

Sherif is the Muslim employee in the Senoussi brothers' butcher shop in Marseilles. He had worked in their business in Algiers and followed them to France with his family after independence.

External distinctions

The linguistic embodiment of ethnic distinction

The Jews' intermediate position between Christians and Muslims in Sétif, acted out in children's games, was also evident in the way in which each ethnic group designated the others. Jews generally referred to Europeans in religious terms; as either 'Catholics' or 'Christians'. The former term distinguished Protestants from the rest of the European population, probably because of their neutrality within the then-current anti-Semitic climate. What this religious terminology emphasizes is the importance of religious ascription in the ongoing ethnic game in colonial society. Christians would also be called either 'Frenchmen' or 'Europeans', this designation underlining a relevant distinction in this small town where the European population included Italians, Swiss, and Spaniards who had acquired French citizenship in the late nineteenth century. The term 'Frenchmen' had the advantage of isolating French culture as the ruling one in the local cultural landscape.

Jews used various terms to designate the Muslim population depending on their current relationships.[17] The term 'Muslim', a rather respectful term founded on religious ascription, is used when narratives mention religious differences such as those related to the celebration of religious festivals. It designates a close Other, a respected neighbour with whom one has good relationships and cultural affinities. The term 'Arab' is a generic one, sometimes even including the Kabyle Berbers who made up a small part of Sétif's population,[18] and thus represents the ultimate otherness. In addition, the Jews borrowed derogatory terminology from colonial ideology, undoubtedly to underline the differences in social and political status between themselves and the Muslims. In this meaning system the latter were called 'indigenous' (elsewhere translated into 'native'), as if the Jews themselves were denying their own nativeness in this country where their ancestors had been present for centuries, even before the Arab invasion. The characterization of Muslims as 'natives' symbolically extracted the Jews from their local ancestral context, as if they were already contemplating emigration. A similar symbolic process was at work in the ultimate derogatory designation of Muslim women as *mouquères*,[19] a term evoking patriarchality as the bastion of archaism in Muslim native society.

The terminology used by Muslims to designate their Jewish neighbours also points to the status of the Jews in Setifian multiculturalism. In Arabic, the only language spoken by most women, Jews were called *yehudin*, a term traditional in the Muslim world for designating both the ethnic and the religious dimension of Jewishness. Muslim men speaking French would call the Jews 'Israelites', in accordance with French ideology defining Jewishness as essentially a religious matter. In most accounts, though, the terminology used by Muslims clearly distinguished the Jews from the French: 'On this soccer team there were Israelites but no Frenchmen!' (Bou-Slimo). In the Muslim classification, Jews were not full-fledged Frenchmen and occupied a marginal position in the representation of France as a nation. Muslims referred to Christians as 'Frenchmen', 'Europeans', or 'colonists'.[20] The Arabic term *rwama* (Christians) was rarely used to refer to the French, an indication that they were viewed by Muslims more as a dominant political group than as a religious entity.

The languages spoken by Sétif Jews from the end of the past century until their emigration clearly bear witness to their status as a liminal community. Jews in the Maghreb had spoken Arabic as their everyday language since medieval times. Although this Arabic was different from that spoken by Muslims, their linguistic practices were part of their deep roots in ancient Arabic Maghrebian culture (Chetrit 1980, Cohen 1912, Stillman 1989). After being collectively granted French citizenship in 1870, Algerian Jews had gradually adopted French culture through massive secular education. Towards the beginning of the twentieth century, French became the first language of many Jewish children, whereas their parents, born in the late nineteenth century, continued occasionally to use their ancestors' Arabic. In the early twentieth century, the use of French in family communication indicated parents' desire to provide their children with the means to become integrated into a promising Western society. French began to penetrate family life initially through the naming system. Moshe became Marcel, Sultana became Reine or Reinette (Little Queen), Abraham became Albert. By giving their children French names parents hoped to enable them to find jobs and respectable positions in the dominant French-speaking community in Algeria. As French slowly but steadily became part of Jews' everyday speech, they became bilingual, the qualitative and quantitative role accorded to French or Arabic reflecting their particular positions in colonial society. This complex linguistic policy highlighted the distinction between Jews and, on the one hand, the Christian community which rejected them, and on the other, between Jews and the Arab–Muslim community from which they wished to maintain their distance. As Guy recalls, linguistic dilemmas remained political ones until shortly before Algerian independence: 'We had good relations with the Arabs. And then, the Jew speaks Arabic at home. We can express ourselves better in Arabic than in French, it seems to me. There are some expressions, you'd laugh more in Arabic than if you translated them into French. They would lose their charm.'

In the modern history of the Algerian Jews, the passage from the Arabic lexicon to the French has often been accomplished through translation. In this process, the intent has been to grant symbolic value to an Arabic signified by identifying it with a French signifier. Thus the traditional stew known as *m'khater*, consumed by both Jewish and Muslim families during the festivals of the religious new year, has been translated as *blanquette de veau*: the traditional lamb has been replaced by veal, a high-ranking type of meat, enabling the Maghrebian dish to compete with one of the jewels of French gastronomy (Bahloul 1983). Similar linguistic strategies have been applied to the Hebrew lexicon designating religious festivals and artefacts. Thus the names of religious rituals have been translated to bring them into line with the Catholic religious code. The bar mitzvah, for example, has become First Communion; the spring ritual of Passover, called Pesah in Hebrew, has been renamed Pâque (French for Easter); that of Shavuoth[21] was translated as Pentecôte (Pentecost); and circumcision (*brith-mila*), has become *baptême* (baptism). This translation was clearly a strategy for the legitimation of the Jewish ritual system through analogies with the dominant religious code.[22] While the Sétif synagogue was located off the main street, as indeed was the Protestant church, the Catholic church sat imposingly opposite Square Foch in the heart of a commercial quarter densely populated with Jewish and Muslim merchants.

Linguistic strategies were used by the Jews of colonial Algeria in the pursuit of upward mobility and integration into the dominant society. Language was both a social terrain in which the interethnic and political stakes were high and a register of socioeconomic positioning. Jewish families in which French was dominant in domestic interactions were considered 'progressive' and upper-class. By contrast, families whose interactions were dominated by Arabic communication were judged 'backward' and at the bottom of the social ladder. To show 'progressiveness' one had to perform predominantly and publicly in French. Yet the paradox was that, in a community with a high proportion of lower-class and working people, those who flaunted their use of French were considered by some traditionalists as renegades or hungry for power. Elie Akoun was one of these traditionalists, although he was also one of the few residents of Dar-Refayil to have pursued higher education in Algiers. He recalls:

Learning French was hard for us. We didn't have a rich vocabulary for school essays, compared with those very emancipated Jews who *only* spoke French and who, of course, observed the religion *à la française*, because the two went together. These Jews were very emancipated, like the Zermatis [the Jewish colonists in town], for example. They no longer spoke Arabic, it was shameful for them. They only spoke French, and a polished French. For the Zermatis, there was only the subjunctive![23] He was a prominent attorney and president of the local bar association. There were some Jews, like Chicha, for example, who were tax officials. During that time, you needed solid credentials, . . . a law degree. They lived in villas or in rich-looking apartment, for example, buildings on the Rue de Constantine.

These strategies for linguistic legitimation of social status (Bourdieu 1982:23–58) were also common in lower-class circles where Arabic was used in daily and domestic communication, but here they were aimed at Muslims. The Arabic spoken by Jews claimed to be more literate and more polished than that spoken by Muslims:

I spoke Judaeo-Arabic to my children. It is not the same Arabic, it was the Jewish. They [Muslims] did not speak Arabic the way we did. When you said to an Arab, '*Eydji!*' (Come!), he wouldn't understand. For them it would be '*Arwa'h!*' Also, we say '*Galu*' (He says), but they say '*Qalu*'. This was the Judaeo-Arabic of the Constantine region. Ours was closer to literary Arabic!   (*Zahra*)

Though it was a handicap to their emancipation, the use of Arabic made it possible for the Jews to maintain close links with the Arab population, particularly in their commercial exchanges. At the same time, because it was spoken only in the most intimate social settings – family life, ritual, and joking – it rooted the Jews in their ancestral Maghrebian traditions in private life, whereas French was meant to propel them towards modern Western life in public. In this the linguistic practices of Jews in colonial Algeria were like those of colonized populations elsewhere. Social and cultural domination operates mainly through language, and only social groups of intermediate status (such as mestizos, immigrants, and minorities) are able to acquire access to the dominant culture through its language (Fanon 1952).

Recollections recorded in the 1970s still displayed scattered Arabic phrases. Memory here uses language as a narrative strategy: the appearance of an Arabic term or phrase always indicates a semantic shift to the register of intimacy. The occasional use of the Arabic lexicon in narratives delivered in French is a form of re-enactment of past experiences: just as reconstructing the past requires rebuilding the past house, so it requires a return to past linguistic practice. Arabic often appears in narratives to denote positive emotional and comforting experiences. Some examples are 'The house was full of *sôl* (festive atmosphere),' 'We'd give it [the tree] the *'ers* (festive look),' and 'He [the father] told her, '*Ester'ha*' (Protect her).'

The marketplace for ethnic exchanges

Jews and Muslims thus communicated in Arabic both in domestic life and in their commercial exchanges. Shopkeepers and artisans conducted business in the same area, to the south of the Rue de Constantine: they were spatially close. Jewish memories rationalize the use of Arabic in terms of the need to maintain business relationships with the Muslims. But in this society where everything was negotiated, as in other Maghrebian societies (Rosen 1984), commercial exchanges led to a certain degree of interdependence, reciprocity, and balance between the two dominated communities. This state of affairs lasted until, at the peak of the war of independence, there was no longer any affinity between them.

Moushi Senoussi was familiar with these exchanges of goods and services. As a butcher, he negotiated the purchase of livestock with regional Arab breeders every week. The cattle market, dominated by Arab breeders, was held south of town every Tuesday. Moushi's semirural background had both economic and social advantages, providing substantial social capital. The Arab cattle dealers respected him and cultivated friendly relationships with him: they too depended on these implicit formal contracts. Yvette remembers how every Sunday night Arab cattle dealers would visit Moushi at home to establish their common accounts. They would dine in Dar-Refayil and then go off to sleep in the *hammam*. During the most critical times of the war and during the 1935 and 1945 riots, they protected Moushi and his family by warning them of imminent danger so that they could take refuge at home as quickly as possible. During the Second World War, the Senoussis and their relatives were never short of food, which was rationed elsewhere in town; Arab farmers supplied them with food in exchange for favourable business arrangements. This reciprocity was so elaborate that Rosette does not hesitate to say that, had there been a Nazi invasion from Tunisia, the Arabs would have hidden the Jews whereas Frenchmen would gladly have handed them over. Jewish memory retains this system of balanced relationships with the Muslims as opposed to the hostility of the French: Jews tell of feeling protected by Muslims until the beginning of the war of independence.

Identity in the stadium

Sports in Sétif provided a dramatic setting for the practical and symbolic expression of the ethnic game. Until independence three soccer teams dominated the scene. The Sporting Stade Sétifien, to its opponents the Three S,[24] represented the French on the field and was managed by local notables, mostly colonists. The Stade Africain Sétifien, the indigenous team, was made up exclusively of Muslims and politically affiliated with the pro-independence Mouvement pour le Triomphe des Libertés Démocratiques. The Union Sportive Franco-Musulmane de Sétif (USFMS) was a Muslim team which included some Jewish players and was managed by moderate Muslim intellectuals. Obviously, the competition between these teams went beyond mere sport. A victory of the Muslim team over the French would be interpreted as the symbolic revenge of the 'natives' over the 'colonists'. According to a former USFMS player interviewed in Sétif in 1980, 'It was war!' In the stadium as in the street, political and ethnic antagonisms took on a theatrical form, but in sport the Jews played a more limited role.

Eddie Senoussi came onto this political-sport scene when he was about sixteen. A passionate soccer fan, he first played on the French team, following his loyalties as a citizen, but there he soon experienced anti-Arab racism and the remnants of local anti-Semitism that had survived the war:

There were anti-Jews [on this team]. They always talked about this. Once we lost a game on a Sunday, so they said to me, 'It's because you didn't go to the synagogue yesterday; you didn't go and pray!' So I went and played with the Arabs, and I stayed with them, the USFMS. I travelled with them. I covered all of North Africa with them, with the Arabs.

On the Arab team, Eddie remembers being respected and protected. He was the only Jewish player on the team. The Senoussis' long-standing immersion in the local 'native' population helped him get along with his Arab team-mates. The Muslims who managed the team saw in Eddie an ally on the soccer pitch and probably in politics, too. His participation had made the team more competitive, and in exchange they tacitly offered the Senoussis and Eddie in particular a whole range of favours. Eddie had numerous entrées into the local Muslim community:

When I scored a goal, they [the managers] would give me money. I was often offered gifts in the street. For example, if I were to go to an Arab doctor, he didn't want to charge me. I didn't pay. When I went into a bar or a pastry shop, I never paid. And when I played I attracted many Jewish spectators and supporters. For them, then, it worked like this: they had an interest somewhere, they'd return it in favours. I just played with them, that was all, but for them it was a service.

The Three S (the 'Catholic team', as it was called at the Senoussis') interpreted Eddie's sports commitment as a political statement: its anti-Semitism had found its justification. The local Jewish community had assumed an ambiguous position in the colonial conflict, shifting from one side to the other. Without his intending it, Eddie's sports activities had become the dramatic representation of the liminal position of Jews in the local sociopolitical landscape.

Practical boundaries: dress, food, and folk medicine
The cultural proximity of Jews and Arabs in colonial Algeria pervaded many domains of their respective and shared cultures, both in private and in public life. Just as language was shaped by the contingencies of modern Algerian history, so were dress, food, and folk medicine. In these, too, sociocultural distinctions were strongly marked, and the politics of ethnic and religious domination expressed itself in a dramatic way. Here again, narrative memories use this domain of cultural expression to circumscribe relationships between Jews and Muslims:

It was warmer with the Arabs than with the Christians. We didn't treat them like slaves. We were always on the same level as they. We weren't prouder than them. The Arabs liked living with us. You have to remember that we had the same customs, the *youyous* [ululations], Arabic music, Arabic dress. *(Marcel and Rosette)*

Though narrative memory persists in grouping Jews and Muslims in the same cultural block, dress, food, and folk beliefs tended to place the Jews in the intermediate position assigned to them by the all-encompassing cultural 'dissemia' characteristic of their engagement in Westernization.[25]

This process was made most visible in dress, especially female dress. By the turn of the twentieth century, Muslim women wore the veil in town and the traditional *gandoura* at home, whilst Jewish women had never worn the veil and alternated between traditional and Western dress. Clothing had been a mandatory distinguishing mark for Jews under Muslim rule since the Middle Ages. Whereas the *gandoura* worn by Muslim women had a yoke and flounces and was drawn in the waist with an embroidered belt trimmed with gold, that of Jewish women was trimmed with gathers and folds and belted with a coloured scarf.

Anna Akoun, born in the late years of the nineteenth century, was familiar with these native dress codes because she had followed them as a seamstress until after the Second World War. Her clientele was exclusively made up of Jewish and Muslim women. Her daughters, who were also seamstresses, had a clientele of Jewish and European women and began to introduce Western dress codes into the trade. Thus the 'Frenchification' of Jewish dress went through the same historical development observed in language. On the whole, the generation born towards the end of the nineteenth century maintained the traditional native dress until after the First World War. At this point traditional dress began to be worn only on more private occasions and for religious festivals, whereas Western dress gradually appeared in social settings involving contacts with French-speaking people. The generations born after the First World War almost completely abandoned traditional dress, just as they no longer spoke their ancestral Arabic. From then on dress differences reflected age and socioeconomic distinctions, just as did linguistic variation. Flaunting traditional dress was displaying reluctance to Westernize and become emancipated socially and culturally.[26] In some Jewish families that clung to patriarchal rule, husbands required their wives to wear the traditional dress because European-style dresses would reveal their legs and because the accessories associated with traditional dress (such as jewelry) constituted a public display of the household's status.

The one exception to this dress dissemia among Jews was the festive attire worn by boys for their bar mitzvah. On this occasion, ritual coming of age was equated with social and cultural coming of age in dress semantics. The generation of Jewish boys who celebrated this ritual after the Second World War also consecrated its entry into European culture through the ritualized display of the Western-style suit:

The day of my bar mitzvah, they [women] dressed me in the morning, with Arabic music, before taking me to the synagogue. I went out onto the owners' balcony in my underwear, and they dressed me in a shirt, singing, and then the trousers and the shoes. They say there's a special song for the shoes. So it was the little grey suit, made of flannel, a very beautiful suit in brushed wool which my uncle had bought in Paris for me, a beautiful suit with short trousers.   *(Elie)*

Food habits followed a similar policy of social and cultural distinction. The food eaten by Jews in Sétif, as in most North African communities, was almost identical to that served in Muslim households except for differences in ritual dietary laws. Food exchanges were frequent between Jews and Muslims. Muslims would eat in Jewish homes, but the reverse was less common because of the greater number of dietary prohibitions in Judaism. Some Jewish families were persistent in maintaining their food customs, their *'ada*, which were governed by their geographical and historical origins. It was typical to serve traditional cuisine for ritual meals and French-style cuisine for ordinary ones (Bahloul 1983). A similar logic governed the use of traditional items such as the *kanoun* to cook ritual meals and European-style implements for everyday cooking. The entire universe of bodily practices was sectioned off by barriers that functioned in the local community's hierarchy.

Folk beliefs followed a similar symbolic and practical logic. Those relating to medicine and sympathetic magic had long been favourable ground for exchanges between Jews and Muslims. Despite the scorn of local Frenchified elites and the rabbis' opposition, indigenous populations persisted until recently in their belief that 'Arab' medicine was more efficient than Western medicine in the treatment of specific illnesses. Folk medicine had great expertise in some types of mental disorders and in illnesses threatening family fertility.

As in other rural societies of the Mediterranean and southern Europe, the therapeutic personnel were predominantly female, as if women had made themselves the keepers of the community's social and biological reproduction. Thus female folk medicines were considered efficacious for treating 'nervous breakdowns' that culminated in possession crises attributed to the influence of the *djnoun* (sing. *djinn*). Healers were called to help end prolonged sterility or spinsterhood. They were experts in children's diseases, which were quite common until recent times, as indeed was infant death. Finally, they were believed to be able to warn families about the dangers of an ill-fated alliance or to restore conjugal balance when such a marriage had taken place.

Folk therapeutics not only helped comfort troubled families but also allowed the social 'recycling' of spinsters or widows in these much-needed and respected community roles. Practising folk healing allowed women disadvantaged by spinsterhood or prolonged widowhood to recover their respectability in the community. Marginalized because of a meagre dowry or because their husbands' death had left them impoverished, these women would become, thanks to their therapeutic talents, indispensable to the maintenance of local family oriented values. Some of them had made the practice of folk healing their only livelihood.

Gilda, for example, though she had been married to Moushi at the age of thirty-two (a belated marriage by the standards of 1937) and had hardly any education, acquired a good reputation and a substantial clientele among Jewish and Muslim families. It was Ma Sultana, herself an impoverished widow, who had passed on to Gilda the secrets of folk medicine. Everyone in Dar-Refayil respected and protected Ma Sultana because of her healing skills. She is said to have been very old, almost a hundred when she died – memory having made her a saintly figure through the narrative combination of poverty and longevity. According to some accounts she was immortal. Hadn't she 'died three times', women said, and awakened while everyone was praying over her dead body?:

Ma Sultana died in 1956. She was very old. She was everyone's granny. For us, she was the soul of the house. If a child was sick, she was the one who looked after him. She would massage him and cure him. She had the know-how. She even served in deliveries; they'd come to get her. When someone was sick, she'd go and look after him. She'd cure him. If a child had a sore throat, she'd massage him and the next day he would be fine. She had good hands, as they say.

Poor woman, she lived all alone. Her last years were awful. In the middle of winter, her door would be open, and we'd hear her screaming in her bed. She must have suffered a lot, the poor woman! She was a saint. She went straight to paradise. And thus she had a splendid funeral. It was her great-grandchildren and I who lowered her into her grave. And it was a kosher grave, dug by young Jewish men.

(Zahra)

Folk medicine in Sétif was women's business. It granted them parallel authority legitimated only in female networks. Men's memories display disdain for a practice that they characterize as the product of ignorance. It is clear that these healers' major concern was to protect the family as an institution, a role that they assumed in many other domains of their lives. Paradoxically, it was often women who had experienced family tragedies who were charged with this important task. Female folk medicine operated as a social regulator and tended to strengthen, on the symbolic level, the fragile fabric of patriarchal society. Women thus employed illegitimate authority to protect an institution in which they were deprived of legitimate authority (Bourdieu 1980:323–4).

Within the domain of folk medicine was expertise in dealing with the *djnoun*, which threatened children's health, conjugal peace, matrimonial projects, and brides' fertility. The story of Alice's marriage tells us how, thwarted by his potential mother-in-law's reluctance, Daniel the butcher had threatened to call for the *djnoun*'s intervention if he were to be refused the hand of the young Alice: 'Well, I'm coming to ask you for the hand of the girl you are raising. But if you turn me down, I don't know what might happen. Because my mother . . . the *djnoun* . . . she'd spit fire!' (Gilda). The belief system based on the concept of the *djnoun* offered a broad range of strategies for dealing with problems beyond the reach of traditional social negotiations. The *djnoun* thus had both positive and negative features: their appearance was interpreted as a warning, but they were also seen as dangerous in themselves. Possession was the *djnoun*'s most common way of manifesting itself. As the managers of folk medicine, women were the most vulnerable to the *djnoun*'s attacks. Women's memories report numerous cases of women's being possessed:

Well, there was one woman who hadn't had a single marriage proposal. She could-n't get married. So she was like this [showing tied hands], 'stuck', *m'ketfa*, tied up as if with a rope.[27]   *(Gilda)*

I saw how a madwoman, a super-madwoman, was cured. She had gone out naked into the street, in just her underwear, and she was a very smart girl. It's the one who married her [own] cousin. I saw her like this, in the street. She was talking to herself, her hair was loose. None of the doctors of Sétif managed to cure her, and the hos-pital was large enough to treat serious illnesses. She was raving mad.   *(Rosette)*

The *djnoun* also revealed themselves in dreams through a symbolic process quite common in Jewish folk belief. Dreams were a favourable place for communication with the *djnoun* and one which would signal potential flaws in the social system (Bilu 1987).

Illnesses caused by the *djnoun* were usually treated by controlled trance guided by the victim's closest female relatives. These therapeutic sessions were known by the generic Arabic term *salha* (relief or reconciliation). Clearly, the idea was to enter into negotiations with the spirits. The most effective techniques for this involved music and dance aimed at calming the spirits' wrath. In some cases, these healing techniques required the intervention of the *Bou-Sa'adiya*, who would accompany the possessed's jerky movements with increasingly rapid drum beats. In severe cases, more aggressive physical techniques had to be used. The aim was to release the possessed body from the spirits' hold. In milder cases such as minor illness or nervous breakdown the patient was put on a spice-free or salt-free diet or on a diet of sweets, pastries, or olive oil. The *djnoun* were said to dislike strong flavours, so their wrath could be calmed only by sweetness. In the same vein, the possessed body would be massaged with olive oil or the victim's house enveloped in clouds of incense. Finally, the healers might suggest placing magical objects around the home to persuade the spirit to release its hold. A mixture of henna, alum, and incense might be placed near the victim's bed or in the room thought to be inhabited by the spirit.

These beliefs were held by both Jews and Muslims in Algeria but were elaborated differently within each community. The Jews would not use any of these healing practices on religious holidays; the *djnoun* were not allowed to interfere with religious fervour or compete with God. Folk beliefs could not compete with the religious canon endowed with supreme value in the native symbolic system. Gilda justifies this hierarchy by claiming that the treatments in which she was expert were not effective during religious festivals. Thus, while less valued than official religious beliefs and subjected to each community's religious particularism, folk beliefs constituted a favourable area of Jewish–Muslim interaction and symbolic exchange. Gilda, for example, had woven a valuable web of symbolic prestations and counterprestations with a great number of Muslim families who had requested her help. In a way, the *djnoun* were used as symbolic negotiators between Jews and Muslims:

There was a[n Arab] cattle dealer whose children never survived. They would die at birth. So when a child was born in his house, I was the one who would name it. Then the [Jewish] shopkeepers would provide clothes for him, because giving clothes was a good deed. And his children did live. So he would bring us walnuts, dates, bread, and even money. He loved the little one [Eddie and Clarisse's first son].

(Gilda)

This system of symbolic (and sometimes material) exchanges proved protective of the Jews during the war of independence; Muslims protected the Jewish families to whom they were obligated through the folk medicine system.

The Jewish community

The boundaries separating the three religious groups in town were consolidated in the Jewish community by a complex and compact network of mutual help and socialization that involved most individual actions. This network made it possible to avoid Jewish–Christian intermarriage, common among the Jews of the larger Algerian coastal cities, until the late 1950s. Up to their very last years in Sétif, the Jews remained a close-knit and supportive community. Membership identity strengthened this vulnerable minority: 'Because Sétif was small, because we knew everything that went on in the Jewish community, we felt it personally when, for example, a Jew had been killed in a terrorist attack. We felt as if it were our property which was being taken away from us' (Guy). This solid articulation of membership identity was bolstered by an active network of educational, liturgical, and charitable organizations, both religious and secular.

Sétif had two synagogues, a Talmud Torah or Sunday Hebrew school, several Jewish youth movements, and a consistory (rabbinical executive board) that was often involved in family matters such as the resolution of conjugal conflicts. These institutions, mostly religious in scope, were attended mainly by men. Women rarely attended synagogue services except on Yom Kippur when they would make a brief appearance. The Saturday morning visit to the synagogue was one of the highlights of Jewish social life and at the same time a demonstrative strategy in the local multiethnic context: making the Jewish community dramatically visible and strengthening its cohesion. Dar-Refayil's men nostalgically remembered a time when Jewish religious ceremonies took place out of doors, in public. After the religious service on Saturday morning, the faithful would invite each other for an apéritif and a bite of their home-made sabbath dishes.

It is, however, the Hebrew school which Guy, Claude, and Elie, teenagers in the 1950s, remember most vividly. Every Thursday and Sunday (days off from school) they went there to learn Hebrew prayers to prepare for their bar mitzvahs. Jewish children never had holidays, Claude insisted, and most of their experiences evolved within their Jewish peer groups. Some children pursued religious education after their bar mitzvahs. The Talmud Torah was a privileged place for children to learn what it meant to be Jewish and to establish social relations within the Jewish community:

The Talmud Torah really shaped our minds. We were spiritually mature compared to *goy* [Gentile] children. We would discuss metaphysical problems whereas *goy* children of our age were still into Santa Claus. We studied Rachi [an eleventh-century Jewish theologian from Troyes]. This had an effect on everyone's social life. For example, a Jewish child would respect his parents more than a Gentile, because we were taught to respect our parents, old people, and the great *mitzvah* [Commandment] of helping others. *(Elie)*

Rabbis exerted considerable authority over the Jews' private life. As in other Jewish communities of North Africa and Europe, their advice was sought to resolve a whole range of family problems. They were the guardians of family unity and, consequently, of the community's demographic stability. One of Sétif's last rabbis, Rabbi Shalom Guedj, was sanctified after his death through pilgrimages to his grave by Sétif's Jews during Lag ba-Omer, the thirty-third day after Passover.[28]

Certain public facilities used by the Jews for religious purposes were not run by the Jewish community. Although the *miqve* or ritual baths were operated by the consistory, the public oven and the public baths were privately owned. Women would take their sabbath *hallah* to the Muslim baker's oven to have it baked in a wood fire, and their Purim pastries were baked collectively there. The collective oven, a necessity for households with no baking facilities, was a key locale for female socialization. The weekly bath taken on the eve of the sabbath or of any religious festival was in fact a ceremony of preritual collective purification. Jewish religious life had appropriated Sétif's multireligious street and inscribed in it its own ritual pace. The community as a whole was involved in the celebration of weddings, because invitations in Sétif were made not by mail but by individual visits to guests' homes. Private life was in the street, say Elie, Guy, and Claude, and religious festivals were 'felt' more than they are in Paris, where the uprooted ritual has withdrawn into domestic intimacy.

These public rituals constituted fertile occasions for the display of the community's mutual help system. In keeping with their privileged status and prestige within the urban community, Jewish colonists would hold annual parties for Jewish families to celebrate the end of Passover food prohibitions: the *mimuna* involved country music and abundant food.

Finally and most important, the community spared no effort in controlling teenagers' leisure. Some of the diversions offered were organized by the community itself, others by informal Jewish social networks. Dar-Refayil youngsters went to Jewish dance parties organized by the community for Purim. It was very rare for Jewish teenagers to venture to attend Christian dance parties, given the rigid Jewish-Christian segregation that persisted in town until the end of the 1950s. Dance parties were thus undoubtedly a form of community control over matrimonial plans and family stability among Jews and an arena for ethnic policy:

We had a much better time when we went to Jewish dances, when we were among ourselves. When we went to other dances, there were always problems with Christians. They would quarrel. But in Jewish dance parties, it was nice, we had fun, we'd all go out together, like that.   *(Eddie)*

We'd go the four of us, Yvette, Eddie, my brother, and I. But if we [the girls] danced once with a friend, even not a stranger . . . so if we danced twice, it wouldn't do. They'd say [the brothers], 'Hey, you'd better cool it! You're going to stop it. If you want to dance, we'll dance with you.' So then we wouldn't move. And they [the dance partners] would come back: 'Would you like to dance?' 'Eh . . . we're not dancing anymore, we're tired.'   *(Clarisse)*

A similar type of ethnic separation existed between Jews and Christians in bars. The universe of bars was highly segregated along ethnic and religious lines. Jews would gather in Jewish-owned bars, avoiding Christian-owned ones which they saw as dens of racism and anti-Semitism. Muslims were practically absent from this network's 'European' sector because alcohol consumption was prohibited by their religion and they socialized within their own networks of Arab cafés. In bars, too, Jewish men would recognize the familiar reference points of the Jewish religious calendar: some bar owners maintained part of their premises for the consumption of kosher food and drink during Passover. Jewish teenagers would go to Jewish bars right after their bar mitzvahs as a sign of their accession to male adulthood. Guy recounts how his father accompanied him on his first visit to a bar and ordered an anisette in honour of his son's entry into the world of responsible men.

Last but not least, this small community enjoyed an impressive network of youth movements of different kinds, religious, political, and purely cultural. The Scout movement was a popular one, represented mainly by the Eclaireurs Israélites (Jewish Scouts). Religious movements consisted mainly of the B'nai Akiba groups. Zionist groups were much less well established locally than other culturally oriented movements. For Guy, joining the Dror, a Zionist group with socialist leanings, meant freeing himself from the family fold and in particular from paternal authority:

> *Dror* means 'free' [in Hebrew]. So we were free to do what we wanted. If you wanted to smoke, you'd smoke. Everyone did what pleased him. It was a movement that suited my taste, since I no longer observed the religion. So I said, 'Dad, I'm a member of a Zionist group, the Dror.' He said, 'What does this mean?' I said, 'It means *free*. We can do what we want.' He slapped me and told me, 'As long as you live in my house, you cannot do what you want!' He felt that his authority was being undermined. He meant that *he* was the boss, the master of house. For my father, Israel did not exist.'

Guy tells us clearly why Zionist movements were not successful in Sétif: they did not support the Jewish family. Instead, they competed with it and challenged it with an ideology insensitive to the Jews' aspirations for socioeconomic advancement: 'On the whole, the Jews of Sétif did not talk about Israel. For them, going to Israel meant never coming back. "If we go to Israel, we'll starve." For them, Israel represented poverty; it meant going to your death' (Guy).

Community institutions in Sétif were thus strongly supportive of the family, bolstering its solidarity, cohesion, and reproduction. This support was mainly motivated by the desire to resist the inexorable demographic decline which the community experienced between the First World War and Algerian independence. Yet Setifian Jewish society was not classless and included a variety of social distinctions. The local middle and upper classes managed community affairs and supported them financially, but very few socioeconomic intermarriages took place. A complex system of religious endogamy combined with social exogamy governed matrimonial practices. As a rule, religious endogamy was virtually exclusive. Jews never married local Muslims and only rarely Christians. Jewish–Christian marriage was possible only by moving to other, more Westernized cities such as Algiers. Local middle-class Jewish families, especially those of wealthy traders who travelled a lot and whose social capital was high, often contracted marriages in remote regions among the out-of-town Jewish middle-class. In this case, religious endogamy was combined with geographic exogamy. The Setifian matrimonial market was particularly restricted for the wealthy. By contrast, endogamy, social, religious, and geographical, was practically total among workers. Most of the players in this market were clerks, artisans, and workers who could not travel long distances to find a spouse and rarely required a dowry because marriage was a priority at any price.

Apart from these distinctions in social status, a number of other differences in customs and in cultural histories dominated the social landscape of Setifian Jewry in the first half of the twentieth century. Many Jews had been born out of town. One of the most prestigious components in this community was made up of Jews from Tétouan: descendants of Jews who had immigrated to Algeria in the late nineteenth century and the early twentieth century. Several of these Judaeo-Spanish families had inherited substantial fortunes from wealthy trader ancestors of British citizenship, and in Sétif they enjoyed the prestige of European continental culture. Genealogical memory retains the ancestors' historical and geographical peregrinations to establish high social status in the present. As iconographic support for a legitimating account the narrator will display an old photograph of a great-grandfather elegantly dressed in a smart suit and bowler who had moved to Sétif for business reasons at the turn of the century.

One of the most salient distinctions mentioned in narrative memories is that which stigmatizes the descendants of the obscure Jews known as the Bahusi or Kra'a – what Guy calls 'people from the backwoods'. Some sources on the history of Algerian Jewry characterize the Bahusi as descendants of medieval Jews who had found refuge from the Arab invasion in the Kabylian high plateau (Bugeja 1928–29, Netter 1852) and had become deeply integrated into the Berber cultural and religious system. They are said to have been Kabyle-speaking, nomadic, and largely vegetarian. About the middle of the nineteenth century they gradually began to abandon their nomadic lifestyle, and some of them settled in Sétif where the local community worked actively to bring them back to a more authentic Hebraic religious practice. In the 1930s, though they had readily adopted local Jewish religious customs and very few still spoke Kabyle, they had also retained some of their distinctive rituals and persisted in identifing themselves with their cultural forebears. It now seems likely that these Bahusi, (from the Hebrew *bahus*, 'foreigner' or 'outsider') were the descendants of Karaite Jews.[29] Large communities of Karaites had lived in south-eastern Algeria during the Middle Ages and later migrated to north-eastern cities (Hirschberg 1974–81, vol. 2:160). Karaism, based on the prime importance of a literal reading of the Pentateuch rather than on rabbinical hermeneutics, had since antiquity attracted many followers among the Berbers (Szyszman 1980:61). The alternative designation of Bahusi by the term Kra'a, hypothetically a Hebrew word meaning 'reading' or 'Karaite', is further support for their Karaite origins. It also bears witness to the ancient tensions between Karaites and local rabbis which led to the marginalization of Jews who did not accept rabbinical authority. In Dar-Refayil, residents who claimed Bahusi ancestry were clearly distinguished from the rest of the domestic community, mainly by their rituals and customs. Thus in the household of Mes'oda, who had married a man of Bahusi descent, a lamb's head was roasted for the Passover seder even after the family's migration to France. Ritual memory in this case bolstered genealogical memory.

In fact, many marriages had taken place between Bahusi and local Jews in Sétif since the early twentieth century. Rabbinical policy at the time advocated the sedentarization of these formerly nomadic Judaeo-Berbers and in their integration into the local rabbinical community. Memory has retained the identification of the family as of Bahusi origin and the practical memory invested in specific rituals. The historical origin of these groups has generally been forgotten, but dim memories of former affiliations bear witness to what was a turbulent history.

4

Domestic time

In Dar-Refayil, they say, 'one had no sense of time.' 'We didn't keep track of time in Algeria,' Guy insists. It is as if, when dealing with time, memory sought to cancel it out, to locate the past in eternity, to give it a dimension of the absolute. Domestic memory does not count time: time is an intangible dimension of remembrance of the domestic space. This remembrance flows like a river that never runs dry, re-creating a world in which objects and gestures are endlessly repeated without interruption.

In Dar-Refayil's narrative memory, time is punctuated by the quotidian use of domestic objects and relationships. It is a slow time, interrupted only by imprecise dates. Its most significant punctuation is by religious rituals or those that structure genealogical history such as births, weddings, bar mitzvahs, and deaths. These are the accents in the rhythm of domestic life. Narrative memory measures them, however, outside time: during festivals, no one looks at a watch or keeps track of time in any way. Thus rituals serve as landmarks of reminiscence. The narration of past celebrations is a verbal family reunion: time in domestic memory is woven into the structure of genealogical history. Interviews collected among the Senoussis were conducted during the Passover celebrations, one of the highlights of contemporary Jewish ritual life. The week of dietary restrictions dictated by this ritual[1] gathered together many of the parents, children, siblings, cousins, uncles, and aunts who had lived in Dar-Refayil. My questions were wrapped in ritual proceedings, becoming part and parcel of the celebration of cultural origins which most rituals stimulate. The recounting of Dar-Refayil's story took on some of the sacred character of the gatherings. It was delivered as a commemoration. Its stylistic form and its emergence in the unfolding of personal interactions gave it a religious dimension wherein myth intermingled with history:

There was a man from Algiers, a salesman, who was on a boat the night before the eve of Passover, when they clear away the *hames*.[2] He was on a boat, and all of a sudden he remembered it was the day before the eve of Passover. He was from Algiers,[3] and he said to the waiter, 'Would you have any beef, lamb, or veal liver? It's my custom to eat grilled liver [on Passover eve].' Provided that there is smoke, we need to eat grilled meat that night, because before they [the Hebrews] left Egypt they ate a quick meal, so they lit wood fires and ate grilled meat.   *(Marcel)*

As it does here, the narrated recollection of the house most often unfolds spontaneously along with multiple ritual procedures, verbal, gestural, or iconographic. Memory is ritualized and emphasizes the ritual density of the reunion. My intervention had only a slight effect on this symbolic process; rituals involving large family gatherings had long stimulated the outpouring of memories of Dar-Refayil. It was as if remembrance of the house were a structural part of the ritual – as if ritual were itself a form of communication with the past. In this spirit, images of rituals as they were celebrated in the house appear as reflections of the past in narratives. As in the structure of myth, the memorial narrative is thus associated with ritual drama to produce a performative structure of memory (Bauman 1977, Bauman and Sherzer 1989). In this context, however, the communicative rhetoric is not only linguistic but primarily social. Verbal exchanges, liturgical forms, iconographic performance, and the texture of family reunions constitute an integrated system of meaning whereby ritual dramatizes the memory of the house. My hosts made this clear from the outset when they began their recollections by evoking the festive atmosphere in Dar-Refayil.

One of the important dimensions of this rhetoric is its linguistic articulation. The emergence of recollections in the ritual context stimulates the use of Arabic, which was more often employed in daily exchanges in the past than after the emigration to France. This linguistic reunion is in itself a commemoration: it celebrates a language and the social and cultural context in which it was then frequently used. The complexity of the household's history and its plural nature are imprinted in the code shifting and the subtle combination of Arabic words, their French translations, and Hebrew terms. Different cultures, beliefs, and languages come together here but are sharply distinguished. Ethnic memory is thus clearly multilingual; words and phrases in Arabic, Hebrew, and Judaeo-Arabic occur from time to time in a French-dominated narrative. Recourse to Arabic or Hebrew is used to evoke rituals and their components (names of ritual procedures, dishes, or kitchen utensils). It may also emerge in the recollection of past verbal exchanges. Thus one might say; 'My father went to visit my mother-in-law-to-be and told her, *in Arabic*, '*ester'ha*'' Past social life is re-created in past language. The use of the past language, almost completely obsolete in everyday communication, constitutes a form of *representation* of the past and in this sense is part and parcel of the performance of memory. Just as poets resort to an ancient (one might say primitive) form of language, so the poetics of Dar-Refayil's memoirs uses the language of origin in its representation of the past.

The very close association of ritual and memory brings us back to the reproductive function of ritual. Ritual in its performative structure and its association with religious categories allows participants to place themselves in history and geography. Though the ritual system here is governed by the conventions of universal Judaism, it is inscribed symbolically in the immediate Maghrebian past. It is thus made contingent on and rooted in a specific historical and geographical context through memory. In this process, it works as a system of cultural reproduction: religious rituals are occasions for the strengthening of family ties, those essential ties celebrated by collective memory when it re-creates the domestic universe in which they were daily woven. Ritual and memory in tandem therefore proceed to erase time symbolically by gathering different generations of relatives in the same discursive event. In narratives emerging during ritual celebrations, the narrators are related to those who listen and to those who are recalled. Memory inscribed in ritual effects the reunion of the members of the extended family, the living and the dead, against and beyond history. Although it refers to a specific Maghrebian history and geography, time is here replaced by genealogical structure.

Embodied time

Time in domestic memory is made up of odours, images, and objects. It is materialized and closely associated with the concrete use of the household's space. It is imprinted in memory through what Halbwachs called the 'influence of the physical surroundings' (1980:128–30). This sense-based dimension is particularly striking in recollections of religious festivals and the major rituals of the life cycle. Festival time is out of time: dates of weddings and bar mitzvahs are rarely provided with any degree of precision and can be tracked only through other, more important events. Festival time is 'felt', and 'seen' in the street, in the household's singular atmosphere, and in the exchanges that take place in it. Remembering religious rituals is also a recollection of the major differences between ethnic communities in colonial Sétif. The ritual in the street, in men's attire in the synagogue, in the food purchases preceding celebrations – all these images are assembled in memory to signify a religious and ethnic identity. This uprooted memory is thus essentially punctuated by sensory and ritual difference – a memory of senses, an *'embodied' difference*:

We'd feel and smell Friday nights back there. It wasn't like here in France: here you don't really *see* the *shabbath*.[4] But in Algeria, you'd *feel* it. Early on Friday, everyone would go to the Turkish bath. Women would go there on Friday afternoon. In households, one could smell the odour of food cooking, that good food which we wouldn't cook during the week; those dishes simmered slowly, while during the week, well, we'd eat anything. But we'd feel it. First of all, the housewife was clean. You could see it just from that. Everyone would be clean. Indeed, you could see the festival.   *(Guy)*

Festive food is granted a preferred status in this litany of sensory memories. It is through festive food that odours and senses are imprinted in memory. The sabbath, Purim, and Pesach are the festivals that best illustrate this process. The *t'fina*, a dish cooked slowly overnight on Friday, is described as the materialization of the slow pace of sabbath time. Its flavour and thick consistency are presented as the gustatory representation of sabbath time in abeyance. Narrators revel in the recollection of the way it was prepared and its presence on the *kanoun* from Friday afternoon to Saturday lunch. The cooking of the *t'fina* holds time in abeyance; it reverses time. Mention of this dish is most often made in evoking the absence of time reckoning in Algerian life. During one of those Friday afternoons in the 1950s, the house's teenagers used the collective sense of suspended time to concoct a hoax that no one would forget:

One day, Charlie, Elie, and Robert played a joke. The Senoussis had cooked the *t'fina* and left it in a corridor to which everyone had access and which led to the balcony. All the Jews would put their *kanoun* in this corridor, and they would leave their *t'fina* there all night long, simmering away on a very low heat. One Friday (everybody would go out on Friday nights), the youngsters ate all the *t'fina* and put pebbles in the pots. Everybody suspected that they had done it.   *(Guy)*

They talk about sabbath time as if it were time out of time – a time of absolute cleanliness, sanctiying bodily purification, and frantic house cleaning, because 'all the brass had to shine'. Sabbath time was also a time of intensified conviviality as dense and rich as the food that was served. Recollections closely associate the richness of festive food with the gathering of family and friends. The Setifian sabbath, like all other major religious festivals, was devoted to the collectivity, and therefore it is at the centre of the collective remembrance of the house. Memory of the festival and its rich foods unfolds as a recollection of the conviviality that was the spirit of the house.

The memories' scenario starts on Thursday with the weekly shopping in the marketplace, which women engaged in together, frantically alternating errands with housekeeping chores and cooking preparations. At dusk on Friday, the men would come back from the synagogue with friends they'd invited for a drink. Women would offer samples of their sabbath cuisine; sabbath food is to be shared, and the sharing is remembered as another symbol of family and community cohesion:

They would also give food to the poor. I remember that every Friday night, I would take some of her [my mother's] *shabbath* food to a rabbi's wife who had lost her husband and lived alone. Before dusk, my mother would prepare her bread, her meatballs, and her couscous. When I came home from school, she would prepare her basket, and I would take it to her. And before I left her, she [the rabbi's wife] would put a coin in my hand.

(Aimée)

The memory of sabbath conviviality also highlights an essential community value in this house, namely, the obligation to invite lonely and isolated people or visiting relatives. After dinner, sabbath time in abeyance was devoted to family leisure: young women's chatting, children's gathering around parents telling fairy tales and the story of the *tsh'ha* (a grotesque character in Jewish folktales of the Maghreb).

Remembrance slows the pace of ritual time: remembered people and gestures appear in slow motion in the calm and settled space of the house. By contrast, what happens outside of this ritual time, just before and just after it, is described rapidly unfolding. The descriptions of the period leading up to a festival are speeded up, as if time itself were in a hurry to get to the celebration. Accounts of festive preparations picture women bustling about the stoves and brandishing dusters, cooking here and cleaning there in a collaborative enterprise. In passing, one might recall the haste of the ancient Hebrews departing from Egypt.

Recollections of rituals follow the yearly cycle of the religious calendar, beginning with Purim. Once again, accounts of gastronomic activities dominate the memories. One remembers the circulation of home-made pastries around the Setifian community as the focus of the preparations. The use of the plural 'we' in these recollections once again suggests that the tradition was one involving female collaboration:

We'd bake our cakes in a special oven. We'd spend the entire day at the oven. The day of the fast of Esther was the day for the *biscuit de Savoie* [sponge cake], and there was a competition for who could bake the most beautiful cake. That was the custom. We'd eat this cake to break the fast. We'd make six or seven of them, and we'd beat up the eggs by hand. And they were such beautiful cakes!

My Aunt Mes'oda was the specialist. She'd bake thirty kilos of pastry at a time.

She keeps up this habit to this day. You'd think she was still in Algeria; you would-
n't know she was in France. She doesn't know how to bake just *one* kilo; she buys
thirty kilos at a time. In Dar-Refayil, each family would bake twenty kilos of pastries. Do you realize what it was like to bake all that? And to fry the *makrud*
[cookies made of semolina filled with spiced dates] on the *kanoun*? And then we'd
start the day of the *ka'ak*, the crown-shaped cookies. And the following day was
devoted to another pastry.   *(Clarisse)*

After the baking came the distribution of the pastry among the family's
relatives and friends. Children were at the centre of these exchanges, being
sent to deliver the packets from door to door – serving as the purveyors of
ritual food, the messengers of the ritual. In each home visited, they would
be given a coin by the housewife, who would return the plate full of her
own home-made pastries. In this broad distribution they were delineating
the boundaries of the Jewish community and of ethnic difference.
Through the circulation of pastry the children were strengthening the
family's and the community's social networks. Remembering the Purim
pastry-making and exchange is another rhetoric of nostalgia for the spirit
of the past community.

Spring is central to memories of cyclical rituals because it involved
major changes in domestic activities and interactions. From mid-March
(the last day of Purim) to the Passover seder there was an endless round of
coming and going. 'We wouldn't get a chance to rest until the first night of
Passover!' one says, to be answered by 'Resting? What about serving up all
the meals and cooking everyday meals during the week of Pesach?' Here as
elsewhere in Dar-Refayil's collective memory, the difference in time and in
people's activities and exchanges is conveyed through images of cooking
and of food flavours and colours. One talks about preserved fruits and
vegetables decoratively displayed on kitchen shelves, another about the
collaborative preparations for Passover in the courtyard – grilling peppers
and tomatoes, grinding peppers for the *ahrissa* [purée of chilli peppers],
cutting up cucumbers, cauliflower, beet roots, and carrots to be pickled in
brine and vinegar, preparing orange marmalade.

Among the active recollections of Passover ritual time are endless discussions on the controversial theme of the definitions of *hames* and
kosher. Memories reactivate this debate, which essentially opposes lineage
customs, so that these discussions evolve as discursive processes of family
identity. Each family has its own interpretation or its own custom, and
arguments about them unfold in Talmudic form. One of the major questions at issue is whether chicken is to be considered kosher or *hames*, some
saying *hames* because of the chicken's granivorous diet. Again, some

consider all legumes *hames* because they swell during the cooking process as does leavened food, and the chick-pea in particular is banished because its Arabic designation, *hamos*, is phonetically too close to *hames*. Some families use sugar in their coffee, while others would sweeten it with dates:

Customs were very important for us. We'd say: 'Ooh! The *'ada*, if you don't follow it [you'll be in trouble]!' Even if the ingredient was expensive, you had to make a sacrifice and get it. That's because we were deeply attached to customs. We were raised like that by our grandparents. We maintained these things, and we were frightened of superstitions. In Sétif, there was a family that kept a cow for milk. They fed her kosher food so that her milk would be kosher. So every morning children would take their milk jugs there and get kosher milk from Mrs. Z.   *(Rosette)*

Rosette's account distinguishes between the Setifian past, when the Jews would observe their family customs and dietary laws, and their present experience, in which ritual prescriptions have lost their importance. The past ritual system is thus reconstructed as a time of absolute cleanliness and religious fervour while the present is considered polluted. In addition, the emphasis on the past importance of customs and religion is a discourse on the modernization of the Jews: Rosette suggests that these customs belong to an archaic world which has vanished since their migration to France.

By contrast, Elie expands on the concept of the *hames*, arguing that the term includes the representation of the devil and therefore its exclusion from the domestic world during Passover is a symbolic return to paradise. Remembrance of the observance of the *hames* prohibition involves a concept of time and its relation to religious and ethnic identity: 'Passover is a week apart. We'd be eager to eat our matzos.[5] It's true, we enjoyed them, not like today' (Clarisse).

Passover time is described as unfolding slowly. It is remembered as a calming time that strengthened domestic solidarity and interaction. The narration of the making of leavened bread is particularly significant in this respect: starting with the imagery of energetic labour, it develops into a picture of cooperative baking:

We'd make our own Passover matzos. Each family would make six or seven kilos. We'd make them round and flat.   *(Zahra)*

So we had to help each other. We'd go to Little Mouna's [down in the courtyard]. We'd have to wait until it rained. Then we'd have to put a can of water outside and let the water sit there overnight. The water had to spend a night under the stars to be kosher, because it was said that we had to collect the water of the rains of *Nissan* [the seventh month] and keep it to bake the matzos . . . And the next day we'd prepare the dough. We had to moisten it gradually, adding water, salt, no yeast . . .   *(Clarisse)*

Each family would bake five to six kilos. We'd get together and say, 'Today we'll make your ration.' At Yvette's, they didn't bake their own matzos, so Little Mouna would come and help us, and my Aunt Esther would, too. One of us would moisten the dough, another would bake it on the *kanoun* using the *tadjin*, the large round board, and we'd call the *kanoun* the '*tabona*', a special one for Arab flat bread. The *tabona* was different from the usual *kanoun* because it was larger. So, as I told you, one woman was in charge of the baking, another supervised the dough because it wasn't supposed to rise, so little by little she'd keep it moist. Another woman sat before a large brass tray supported by cushions upside down over her lap and rolled out the dough and flattened it with a metal stick. So the one would start, then pass it on to the second one to finish and put it on the *tadjin*. The dough wasn't supposed to rise. . . . And the next day, we'd do it again for another family . . . It was a cooperative. But in my mother's time, they'd go to the communal oven and they'd bake their own matzos there. They'd get several families together. But *we* baked them at home, in our apartment or at Little Mouna's.   *(Clarisse)*

In addition to the recollections of cooking traditions as embodiments of past ritual time, narrators often evoke Passover time through the obligation of house cleaning. What emerges from these memories is a domestic space on the move, a room-to-room nomadism as the cleaning gradually covered all the household space and its residents were driven to the margins, the courtyard and the balcony:

So for the entire month [before Passover], we had to clean the house. We had to take everything out of the house and put it in the courtyard. We'd clean and we'd gradually bring everything back in. My Aunt Esther would live for a month on the balcony so she wouldn't dirty her house. Her rooms opened onto the balcony, and there was a laundry room there, so during the month before Passover, she'd live there. She'd clean her house and then she'd close it up. They'd only go back in at night; they'd wash, they'd sleep, and the next morning she'd make up their beds. They'd eat in the laundry room. When the weather was good, they'd eat in the balcony. In our time, we'd wear rags so we wouldn't dirty our clothes, so that there'd always be clean clothes in the wardrobes, well-ironed, all neat. We'd use the oldest dishcloths and leave the well-ironed ones clean and tidy. And when Passover came, then we'd take out and use whatever we wanted.   *(Clarisse)*

The result of this purifiying nomadism in memorial narratives is the activation of domestic exchanges between women, men, and children. This great house cleaning strengthened collective ties within the Jewish sub-group in the house. The house purification is a theme associated in memory with the strengthening of community and ethnic ascription. The purified house is a metaphor of community reunion, the embodiment of the purification of the social order (Douglas 1966). The scenario of house cleaning follows the structure of matzo baking:

So one woman would start, and on the same day the others would follow. One would make the others eager to start. We were used to doing this all together. Girls didn't go out to work. When you did a really thorough cleaning, you practically pulled the house apart. The crockery was scrubbed, all the brass, too. Each woman would put her brass and pots out in the sun. We'd turn out our bedding, refill the mattresses, air the blankets. All Jewish families would have their mattresses restuffed during spring cleaning. We kept the mattress makers happy! After that we'd get the painters to make sure the house would be beautiful and clean and strictly kosher. For Passover we'd wash the crockery and put it back. But we wouldn't use this crockery from one year to the next. We'd just get it out to eat our matzos and the kosher food for Passover. And in the courtyard we [the women] all shared, we'd whitewash our own corners. Each woman would clean up the front of her room. The balcony upstairs at Gilda's, along the balcony – we'd whitewash the whole length of it ourselves.

(Little Mouna)

At the end of this absolute purification, the ritual of *b'dikat hames* involved a symbolic verification that there were no fermented substances in the home. Leavened flat bread made of leftover semolina was baked for the occasion, and samples were placed around each home. The head of the family would pick them up the day before the festival and recite blessings over the clean space. Then, in a spectacular gesture of symbolic discarding of the 'abominable' substance (Douglas 1966), everyone would burn these little pieces on the upper terrace, as close as possible to the sovereign sky.

In women's memories, ritual gestures and foods embody the slowing of the domestic pace and the strengthening of family ties. By contrast, male remembrance is oriented more towards the public dimension of the ritual, namely the gatherings at the synagogue, but even for men the house's odours and flavours cross the boundaries of the domestic space and move to the street during festival time. Family and domestic rituals were visible in the street, they insist, as if the entire street became a domestic world during Jewish holidays. The descriptions of the high holidays' celebrations are a significant illustration of this symbolic process, as memory principally retains the public aspects of the ritual: the large gatherings of Jews in front of the synagogue on Yom Kippur and the ritual slaughter of poultry by specialized rabbis either at home or in front of kosher butcher shops. To affirm this community dimension of the new-year ritual, tradition required each family to sacrifice an additional chicken for the poor. Remembering this detail of the ritual is part of the rhetoric of nostalgia for a vanished community.

The remembered time of the ritual fuses the private and the public. Men emphasize this aspect by differentiating the ritual celebrations in Sétif, public and communal, from the timid, intimate reunions of the family in

Marseilles and Paris. Thus memory of the past ritual is also articulated as a discourse on cultural change and the effects of migration. The religious practice of Jewish families in Dar-Refayil was a flexible religious one, and therefore the recollection of religious festivals does not perfectly conform to the religious canon. The major holidays of the calendar, such as Passover, Purim, and Yom Kippur, are more meaningfully imprinted in memory than minor ones such as Shavuoth or Hanukkah. The former is essentially characterized by the reading of the Ten Commandments in the synagogue, while the latter is mainly marked by the consumption of fried pastries at each meal of the festive week.[6]

Another relatively minor religious holiday, the festival of Yithro, also known as Siyon, was celebrated a few weeks before Purim after the reading of the biblical passage mentioning the reunion of Moses with his father-in-law (Exodus 18). Narrators would refer to this ritual to identify the customs of the families of Bahusi origin.

Genealogical time

The reconstruction in memory of the original house resembles in many ways the design of a genealogical tree. It is as if the house were made the material representation of extended-family ties and history – as if it were the objectified support of genealogy. The house's story is evidently a family story. Time in Dar-Refayil's memoirs is slow and long, its rhythm established by the key moments of the life cycle, landmarks in genealogical time. When narrators have difficulty remembering the date of an event, they mark it out by its proximity to a wedding, a birth, a bar mitzvah, or a death. In large families like the Senoussis, the Akouns, or the Bakoushes, very few years went by without a major ritual in the life cycle. The house sheltering these celebrations provides a material anchor to the remembrance of these key celebrations. Part of this rhetoric consists of remembering that Jean-Louis's circumcision took place at home, as did the births of many of his elder relatives, and that the bar mitzvahs of Elie, Guy, and Claude were celebrated in the courtyard or on the owners' balcony. The house is the starting point of everyone's life and the place from which lives developed cyclically. It has seen people grow and life flow. Its history is long and evolving. Things as they are remembered seem unchanging because they all unfold in the same place. However, things, people, and their lives do change in Dar-Refayil's memoirs, and it is this change within permanence that memory underlines.

Time in Dar-Refayil's memoirs is long also because it goes back in history with the genealogy to the establishment of the house as a domestic group. Narratives develop on how the Senoussis ended up there – on the genealogical processes that led them to do so. Narratives represent the presence of the Senoussi family in Dar-Refayil as the culmination of a long history, an ancient family destiny. Even though, in practice, the whole domestic group lived there only for some three decades, its narrated history in the house expands to cover over half a century. The house's narrated history is endowed with temporal depth because it is built on genealogical structures. Its logic is supported by genealogical memory.

Two types of personal events dominate genealogical narratives: weddings and bar mitzvahs, the former being almost exclusively the province of women and the latter entirely that of men. The two events are similar in their ritual processes and in the way in which they are remembered. Yvette points out that the boy being blessed in his bar mitzvah is called 'hatan' (groom). Events sanctifying masculinity thus stand out in the corpus of descriptions of past rituals. Circumcision is another such ritual, not only celebrating a male's birth but also dignifying and strengthening the symbolic authority of the patriline, and solidifying the community's agnatic spirit. One ritual sequence often mentioned in accounts of past celebrations of circumcision is the naming of the infant in the synagogue on the sabbath following his birth by the whole congregation. Here narratives emphasize the presence of the infant's male relatives – his father, his paternal grandfather, and his paternal uncles, and great-uncles. Circumcisions in Sétif involved the entire community not just the family or the parents. Men's narratives elaborate on this theme, a nostalgic reminder of the agnatic spirit that governed the past Jewish community:

Attending a circumcision was a *misva* [observance of a divine commandment], even without an invitation. They'd announce it at the synagogue; 'Come on, there's a circumcision!' Because children are named at the synagogue. They [the faithful] go up to the *teba* [pulpit], and they announce it. And then, they [the infant's relatives] invite everybody over for an apéritif, a big apéritif. And since everyone knew each other – it was a small place – everyone would come.   *(Eddie)*

Accounts of the celebration of the bar mitzvah follow similar narrative lines. The festivities lasted for nearly a week and consisted in the sanctification of masculinity at each phase. The first phase took place on Wednesday with the blessed bath in the *miqve*, to which the boy would invite his male friends to 'say goodbye to their childhood' as a man might have a stag party before his wedding. A joyful gathering followed the ritual purification and the symbolic haircut, a communal display of the boy's gendering and his introduction into the community of male faithful. As

Guy emphasizes, the bar mitzvah was considered the start of adult life, and its aim was to 'bring the child into the thick of things'. In its last phase, the purified boy and his friends would go off together to smoke cigarettes provided by the boy's father as a way of authenticating his recent entry into masculinity. Alternatively, his male relatives might invite him and his friends to join them in a card game, another very popular form of initiation to masculinity in the Setifian community.

The Thursday was devoted to the boy's *religious* initiation. Before leaving for the synagogue ceremony, female relatives would dress the boy, bustling around him while local musicians played their languorous tunes in the background. Here the boy was as pampered as a bride. Elie's bar mitzvah was celebrated in 1949, the year his Aunt Clarisse and Eddie became engaged, and his recollections of being dressed for the occasion focus on the similarity between the two ceremonies. The celebration of the bar mitzvah in Sétif after the Second World War was as much a social as a religious initiation. It sealed boys' membership in the Jewish community but also their entry into Western society. Today's adult men talk about their bar mitzvahs as if they had been the beginning of their lives as responsible, free men, men in desperate pursuit of emancipation. For Elie the religious dimension of the ceremony was essential, since he continued to pursue religious studies in the following years, but for his friends Claude, Guy, and Little Mouna's sons the bar mitzvah was essentially a social initiation, marking their entrance into the secular world.

Narratives of wedding ceremonies employ an opposite discursive logic. As women's stories, they tell about women's introduction to the intimate and enclosed domestic world. Just as in the descriptions of other rituals, however, the account of the wedding is moulded by the materiality of the domestic space. Each new wedding implied the shrinking of the available living space: the married son took over the conjugal room and the younger children moved out towards the fringes – into the living room, closer to the exit, or closer to the floor. Embodied memory thus recognizes that through marriage a personal status was legitimated which endowed the individual with a valued space in the household. Youngest siblings like Claude retained a vivid memory of this procedure because their older brothers' marriages meant the reduction of their own living space:

When Marcel got married, he didn't stay very long in the house. He had the last bedroom, where only he and his wife slept. No one else slept there. Then there was Eddie, who stayed longer, so we were rather more cramped then. We'd put mattresses on the floor. Aimée and Claire slept on a couch, in the dining room, I think. Yvette often went to sleep at Aunt F.'s house, my mother's [Gilda's] sister. She was not married. She had an apartment a bit farther on, near the market. It took five minutes to get there, and she loved Yvette. She treated her like her own daughter. And Yvette got on well with her, so she'd go and sleep there.   *(Claude)*

Genealogical events have been imprinted on the body because the body experienced them in the first place. Women's narratives about weddings and marriage confirm this logic in emphasizing the ritual dimensions related to the discovery of sexuality, from the wedding night to the religious rules governing conjugal sexual intercourse. Thus Rosette informs us that, in the Setifian tradition, the bride became 'Mrs' after the ritual bath and the civil ceremony. Then the spouses were separated again until the religious ceremony, after which their union was viewed as having really begun. These memories of physical initiation are sealed by the account of the verification of the bride's virginity.[7] This reminded women that their bodies were being placed under the control not only of their in-laws-to-be but also of the entire community. The interests at stake in marriage were those of the entire community, which celebrated itself while celebrating individuals' marriage, thereby providing evidence of its demographic and social solidity and its *biological* continuity.

This collective view of life-cycle rituals is corroborated by the recurrent theme of the invitation to celebrations. This was done in Sétif by word of mouth, never by mail. Direct contact with the prospective guest was in certain kinship situations imperative. Female members of the host family would go from house to house about two weeks before the ceremony to invite various kinds of relatives: 'There were some families, if they hadn't been invited in person, if they had only been invited by telephone, well, they'd be offended. This didn't count as an invitation. You had to go to the person's house. Sétif was small, it wasn't like Paris' (Clarisse). Memory reconstructs this system of invitations to life-cycle rituals as the social representation of genealogical and community cohesion. The invitation implies the collective; it suggests that people were available at any time to attend these celebrations. Outfits and gifts had to be prepared in advance. Narratives materialize this theme through the emphatic description of the reunions in the courtyard or on the balcony, large open domestic spaces structured for conviviality and for communal gathering. Memory tells how the inner world of the house expanded with ritual:

My communion took place in the courtyard. We had large blankets, *hayik*, which we'd hang around to preserve our privacy from the Arabs. So there were big trestle tables, large tables, tiered cakes. It was a really big party. It was like a small wedding.   *(Guy)*

This balcony was very big. We'd hold parties there. All Sétif would come, plus the cattle dealers who worked with my father. And we'd also put up a table in that corner for the poor. All the poor would come, too. (Madeleine)

Genealogical time is thus an embodied time, too: remembrance is built up in the materiality of places and movements. Life-cycle celebrations are landmarks in genealogical knowledge, and at the same time they constitute genealogy *in action*. It is as if they tended 'to construct the notion of [genealogical] *trajectory* as a series of *positions* successively occupied' by the members of remembered group, a 'space . . . in the making and subject to constant transformations' (Bourdieu 1986:71, my translation). The memory of the embodiment of the life cycle is a form of embodiment of genealogy. In uprooted memory, genealogy is not an abstract diagram but an essential structure of remembrance. Objectified in domestic space, it is the perfect representation of the reversal of geographical order: the goal is to erase deracination by re-creating genealogical loci. Materialized in the structures of the original house, it allows uprooted people to inscribe their identity in *tangible*, visible time and space. Objectified genealogy testifies to the dialectic established by memory between the symbolic and the material. The individual's status within the genealogical order is inscribed in the bodily relation to domestic space that is its material metaphor.

The time of Otherness
The objectification of time in the remembered representation of the house is not an indication of a lack of historical consciousness among Dar-Refayil's former residents. This memory is in fact an account of the last three decades of colonial rule in Algeria. Through the focus on spatial remembrance, rather than obliterating history, memory materializes it. As Matteo Ricci taught his Chinese hosts (Spence 1984), remembering is building. The history of Algeria between the end of the 1930s and the early 1960s affected much of the world. Though their stories are part of global history, Dar-Refayil's residents place the house at the centre of this whirlwind of events when they tell us how people there experienced the Second World War and the war of independence. However, this oral history is not merely *histoire événementielle*; the narratives suggest that the upheavals generated by the two wars were latent before 1939, the logical growth of the anti-Semitism that had been widespread in Europe and in Algeria since the beginning of the twentieth century. In Jewish memories, the Second World War was a war against Jews and, more specifically, a war waged by Christians against Jews. According to Eddie, it had all started in

Germany with Kristallnacht. In Sétif it was the local Christians, rather than the Germans, who made war on the Jews:

I left in 1943 to do my national service. We were in the middle of the war. There were lots of Nazi Christians in Sétif, but we did not suffer too badly. They [the Germans] never got to enjoy invading Sétif.   *(Marcel)*

The French! Most Catholics were anti-Jewish! At Haudureau, they found a transmitter which was used to link up with the Germans. Masselot, anti-Jewish, Carbonnel, anti-Jewish.[8] They were all important people with lots of money, and dangerous! If the Germans had come, they would have sold us all, one by one, because they'd already made up the lists.   *(Rosette)*

And the chief rabbi, Rabbi Shalom Gozlan, was the first on their list.   *(Marcel)*

A Christian would have hanged or burned us all, all, all. I lived through Pétain's time, well, pretty lively. I'd have fights at school all the time, and I'd hit the girls as they came out of school. [They'd say,] 'Dirty Jew!' 'Down with the Jews!' 'Long live Pétain!' I can name them all, all the pro-Germans, one by one.   *(Rosette)*

I don't call them pro-German. I just call them anti-Jew, that's all!   *(Marcel)*

Anyway, I can remember it all, I have a good memory. They were just biding their time. . . they couldn't wait for the Germans to come to town.   *(Rosette)*

Obviously, this specific memory of the war has to be understood in the local context of ethnic and religious distinctions. The narrative has a local dimension, circumscribed by the immediate experience of a global phenomenon. This story is one of two sides: the Jews and the Others. Events are reconstructed as critical moments in a long series of antagonistic relationships between Jews and Others. The Second World War is typified by anti-Semitism, i.e. relationships between Jews and Christians. The Algerian war of independence is characterized by the complex relationships between Jews and Muslims. Wartime is time of Otherness, and a time of Otherness construed in terms of the *longue durée*.

One of the critical moments in the World War II narrative scenario was the establishment by the Pétain government of the status of the Jews in 1942. For Algerian Jews in the midst of a long, hard struggle for emancipation, this episode inspired fear that this process might be halted. They had been demoted to 'indigenous Jews', the status they had held before being granted French citizenship in 1870. Denied access to the French school system, they were in danger of sliding back down the social ladder. The closure of schools to Jews is remembered as a major threat because, although the community leaders set up some classes for Jewish children, this system did not work for everyone, and the children of Dar-Refayil did not stay there for long. 'I was at junior school. It is this

Mademoiselle Lazare who said, 'Indigenous Jews, out!' And I used to have a good report every Saturday. I came first at least once a month. I was good in French, in grammar' (Rosette). Rosette's account underlines the paradox of being deprived of French instruction by the French. During the Pétain régime, the dominant cultural model was turned against those who aspired to and excelled in it. The model with which the Jews had identified was now denying them social integration and advancement. Exclusion from the French school system constituted a major interruption to a long story of laborious progress towards Westernization and social advancement, and for some families it caused irreversible damage. In Dar-Refayil, several youngsters were unable to acquire a reasonable level of education in the decades following the war.

In Dar-Refayil's memoirs the Second World War is thus a conflict between the Jews and the French or between the Jews and the West. This dualist view of the war can be found in the recollection of food rationing. Here again a system of interaction between the Jews and their neighbours is indicated. In Sétif, people did not really run out of food if they belonged to a family with sufficient social capital to call in various obligations and debts. Jewish butchers were particularly well placed to barter food. Rosette, an adolescent during the war, explains how her father would bargain for food for his family:

We didn't run short. There was a big shop [across the street], Haudureau, that sold semolina, pasta, and grains. Mr Haudureau, though anti-Jewish, would say to him [her father], 'Sir, I would like a beef filet.' Now, go find a beef filet in Sétif during the war; only billionaires could afford it. [So he'd say,] 'Oh, you want a filet? I've got nine children to feed, so give me a sack of semolina and pasta.' And the next day, 'I'd like some more meat' . . . 'I too would like a sack of flour.' And he would bring up a sack of a thousand kilos of flour, and we had enough food for six months. Whatever happened – restrictions or riots – we had semolina at home to bake bread.

Madeleine, seventeen years old in 1940, worked for a wholesale grocer, a local Jew. With him Moushi would trade meat for groceries and cleaning supplies. By comparison with the situation in large cities like Algiers and Oran, it was relatively easy to find food during the war in small rural towns. Thus cousin Jules, a resident of the capital, sent his son Joseph, then a soldier in the Teleghma regiment, to the Senoussis in 1941 to stock up on food. Eventually Joseph married Madeleine after the war.

Memories of food rationing are particularly eloquent when they evoke the strategies of adaptation and substitution that housewives developed during this period. They had been used to coping with dearth even before the war, so when they were out of coffee they would roast and grind date kernels or chick-peas. When bread was lacking, they would collect leftover pasta, leave it to soak overnight, and knead it the next day. When the American army landed in North Africa in 1942, Sétif Jews were relieved, having watched the German army's advance in Tunisia to about one hundred kilometres from Sétif. They welcomed the American soldiers with open arms and doors. The Americans brought with them canned food, cigarettes, and soap. In exchange, they were invited for dinner, especially if they were Jewish, and from time to time a love affair would develop between a Jewish girl and an American soldier:

Some American troops were stationed in Sétif. So they'd come to visit the families. They'd bring us chocolate and white bread, while we usually ate black bread. John had bought so many things for Odette! Jewelry . . . Odette's fiancé's name was John. There was another one, the one who came to our house. So all the girls wanted to make it with an American . . . Jimmy was the one who came to our house. They were Jewish. They would bring us flour, too. They'd go to the synagogue, and the families would invite them for dinner. And then they'd get into the habit, and they would come and eat with us every day.   *(Madeleine)*

To place the welcoming attitude of the Jews towards Americans in context, one has to be reminded that Roosevelt's army was greeted with hostility by the troops of Pétain's régime stationed in North Africa. While the European population was suspicious or at best indifferent, the Jews welcomed Americans with sympathy and solidarity (Abitbol 1990).[9]

The local contextualization of the narrative about the Second World War takes us back to the historical context of colonial society in Algeria, and therefore the Second World War and the war of independence are closely related in postcolonial memory. The same narrative logic found in the account of the Second World War governs that of the war of independence: the 'events' are narrated through the prism of the complex relationships between Muslims and Jews, now with an additional dimension specific to colonial society, that of the position of the Europeans in this dialogical system. The historical memory of this war goes back long before 1954 and the Algerian nationalist underground army's first attack on the French colonizers. In their analysis of Jewish–Muslim relationships in Algeria, Jewish narratives begin with the incidents of 1935, when a pogrom nearly took place in Sétif, similar to that of Constantine in the summer of 1934. For Eddie, this episode was the beginning of tensions between Jews and Muslims in Sétif. The incidents are described here, however, not simply as the expression of Muslim hostility towards Jews but within the context of the triangular relationships between Jews,

Muslims, and Christians in colonial society. Jewish and Muslim voices concur on the theme that the Christians created discord between the two dominated communities. One of my hosts advanced the famous theory of 'divide and rule'. Ultimately, Sétif's Jewish–Muslim antagonisms are described on both sides as the outcome of Christian anti-Semitism and racism:

It was in 1935, I think, that there were riots against the Jews. It was the Christians who egged on the Arabs. They'd tell them, 'They live there, look there, such-and-such a Jew lives here.' But in Sétif nothing happened. They didn't kill any Jews, because we were shut up. And then the army came.   *(Eddie)*

As a follow-up to this general theme, memories evoke the Arab rebellion that was viciously put down on 8 May 1945. They make it clear that this was directed not against the Jews in particular but against the Europeans in general, even though the most telling recollection of the events is the death of a Jewish girl in the confusion. Despite this, Jewish accounts accentuate the fact that the Jews were protected by their closest Muslim neighbours, coresidents and fellow shopkeepers in the market. One would remember vividly how Arab traders persuaded Moushi, who found himself in the market a few hours before the uprising, to go home to safety.[10] Thus what stands out in the accounts of these explosions of violence is that the Jews did not feel particularly threatened as Jews by the first manifestations of the war of independence.

Things changed in the 1950s. This is the period in which memories locate the beginning of the deep animosity between local Jews and Muslims. The war of independence created an enduring barrier between the two communities, says Guy, who points with bitterness to the Suez crisis in 1956, when, according to him, the Muslim families supported Egypt. Despite this, memories persist in indicating that harmony reigned in the house, primarily because harmony was necessary to each community's survival. This situation lasted until independence, despite the presence in the house of some hard-liners among the young Muslims who were actively involved in resisting French rule. Krimo, Farida's son, and Messa'ud, the son of El-'Ayyashi, the dentist, both disappeared after being arrested by the French military. Elie retained a different memory of this episode:

The leader of the killers was in our house, the son of El-'Ayyashi. He set off a bomb, and I was caught up in the explosion. He came up to me, kissed me, and said, 'I was very sad that you were the one who was caught in the explosion . . . Our families, we grew up together. We've seen you grow up. Really, we're very sorry about this.' We learned afterwards that he was the one who placed the bomb in a booby-trapped car.

The war of independence penetrated the domestic world, although every narrator sought to deny it by presenting an image of harmony and mutual protection. This shows up clearly in the differences between Jewish and Muslim accounts. For young Jews of the time such as Elie Akoun and Guy Bakoushe, involved in Zionist activities or Jewish community militancy, danger crept into their domestic life through the presence of nationalist activists among their closest neighbours. For the Muslim families, danger was most dramatically represented by the house searches carried out by French soldiers looking for weapons and militants. In both cases, the intimacy of the family was disrupted by the eruption of evil, a violation or a pollution of domestic harmony.[11] Jews do not mention the house searches, but Muslims make them the symbol of colonial violence and domination. Thus Amina, Bou-Slimo's daughter, remembers:

They came late at night. Soldiers knocked at the gate, and the owner let them in. They asked for Mr Such-and-such. He showed them the house, and there they took him [Farida's son]. And after he left, we never saw him again; he was dead. He was between twenty and twenty-one. And the same thing happened to El-'Ayyashi's son: they also came to take him at home. They knocked and no one came out. They asked for names, the person's identity, when they searched the entire neighbourhood. They did a search house by house. They looked under the beds, in the fireplace, under the mattresses.

This account suggests in subtle and covert ways that the owner – a Jew – collaborated with the soldiers, showing a veiled antagonism between Jews and Muslims. The situation worsened after 1960. In 1961, the attorney David Zermati, then president of Sétif's Jewish Religious Authority (Cultuelle Israélite), was shot and killed by the nationalist resistance, along with other leading public figures of the Jewish community. The popular Constantine Jewish musician Raymond was assassinated in 1962. The message from the resistance was clear, despite certain intellectuals' reassurances: there would be no room in an independent Algeria for the Jews, as Elie unambiguously explains:

In Sétif, they killed the president of the Jewish Religious Authority. This was not a mistake, we all knew that . . . it was planned to give us a psychological shock by striking at the top. Then it became a rout, everyone ran away; we'd understood. If they'd started to hit important Jews, then we were all for it, and that's what would have happened if we had stayed. Because afterwards, some time later, there was all the stuff about Israel.

By contrast with the descriptions of events in the 1950s, those of the 1960s introduce a new representation into the relationships between Jews and Muslims in the house. Before that time, they resulted from colonial tensions and the anti-Jewishness associated with them. In the 1960s, they were affected by the Arab–Israeli conflict, at least in the representations of Elie and Guy, who had unambiguously chosen their camp. In their accounts the view of Jewish–Muslim antagonism slips from one register to another, from the local to the global context, from one geopolitics, French colonization in North Africa, to another, the conflict in the Middle East. This shift announces approaching migrations, as if narrative were anticipating moving with the people.

Extinction

In this tense situation, two events signal the end of the Jewish epic in Dar-Refayil – two deaths which figure in the narratives as the outcome of two dangers faced by Sétif's Jews at that time. Worn out by the miseries accumulated since Sarah's death, overwhelmed by his sons' departure for Algiers, disquieted by his failing business, Moushi died in March 1960. The narrative of his last days recounts a series of events in rapid succession and, at the same time, a death that seems to go on forever, as if none of his children could accept the inevitable. After a first stroke, Moushi spent some time in the hospital, and the doctors were not sure he would survive. Marcel and Eddie had rushed from Algiers through a countryside rife with ambushes and terrorist attacks. When their father seemed to be a little better, they returned to Algiers, but within an hour of their arrival there Yvette telephoned to tell them that Moushi had died. He had first handed down his responsibilities as head of the family to Marcel, his eldest son:

He couldn't speak much. He could only recognize him with his eyes. When he did speak a little, he went like that [nodding her head]: 'You, you're the eldest son. I want you never to abandon your brothers and sisters. You must always be brave and help them always in every way. You must never abandon them.' So the first thing Marcel said was; 'I'll never set up on my own. I'll take all my brothers with me.' He never wanted to eat his bread alone. *(Rosette)*

An almost biblical vision of the father's death, this reconstruction is a philosophical discourse on the persistence of the patrilineal order. With Moushi's death the epic of the Senoussis entered its last phase in Dar-Refayil and in Algeria. The rest of the Jews in the house would also be swept away in this wave. A month later Polo Bakoushe died, too, and his family, which had left the house in 1958, departed for France. In the Senoussi household, left without a head, Yvette undertook to look after her younger brothers and sisters, and set up house in Dar-Refayil. Fate struck again a few months later, in January 1961, when Jeannot, Yvette's husband, was shot and killed downtown in an FLN attack. Jeannot had been a warden in Sétif's prison, and the uniform he wore to work every day was now perceived as a sign of his collaboration in colonial oppression:

And afterwards, there was Jeannot, just after my father's death. I remember I'd gone to get some coal for the old woman on the balcony, because it was too heavy for her to carry. My mother was downstairs in the courtyard. She was talking with the Arabs. They told her, 'You know, Jeannot, he's been killed.' We were both there alone. I'd just come back from school. And she said to me, 'You know, they say Jeannot has been killed.' So I began to cry. I said, 'It's not true, it's not true!' And Yvette was at work, she was pregnant with Jeannette, and no one wanted to tell her he was dead. So our cousin H. told her, 'Perhaps he's only wounded.' She said to my mother, 'You should take a bed from one room and lay him on it.' My mother couldn't do it. She was crying and trembling. So the Arab women got together and did everything, because the corpse had to be laid out on the ground . . . Bichon, his nephew, had a dog, and he said to his dog, 'Come on, we're going to see Uncle Jeannot.' And they followed him, and then they saw two young men shooting at him, and he fell. The nephew was there when his uncle died, and he was the one who told us all. He was killed by a young man of eighteen. There was a misunderstanding with the prisoners. He was not the one to be killed; it was another guard who was very nasty with the prisoners, and they wanted to take their revenge. And Jeannot was the only one to wear the warden's uniform. He'd say, 'I have nothing to be ashamed of, I'll wear it.' He wore it, and he was killed. In the house, we were not at odds with the Arabs when this happened. They couldn't believe it either.

(Aimée)

These two deaths follow the same narrative logic. Economic vulnerability and the erosion of his family had killed Moushi; the social vulnerability of the Jews had killed his son-in-law. Although narratives present these two deaths as having suddenly undermined the house's harmony, they also display them as the realization of its destiny. Soon after Jeannot's death, Marcel, Eddie, and Madeleine (who had moved to Algiers after marrying Joseph) all encouraged the devastated Yvette to join them in Algiers with her brothers and sisters 'because, they said, there is no man in the house any more'. The family had been beheaded. The last Senoussis left the house in 1961, thus concluding the last chapter of a domestic epic marked by petty miseries and brave but vain achievements.

Little Mouna and her children were the last Jews to remain in the courtyard, and the Akouns were still on the upper floor. Until their departure in 1962, their narratives tell of a gradual dimming of the house's lights. Dar-Refayil had become funereal, a place of absence and of awaited departure. In Denise's account, this period is represented by the metaphor of a light going out:

In this large house with all these people . . . [gone]. We had no light in the courtyard or in the corridor. [When they were there], just having their doors open would give light to the courtyard and in the corridor. But they started to leave; there wasn't any light left. Not only was it dark, one couldn't see, but it was spooky, too. We were the last ones, and from then on, it was all over. I couldn't wait to leave.

Epilogue: memory re-creates links

The Senoussi family emigrated together to France in 1962. Madeleine had left a few months earlier for Nice with her husband and two daughters. Charlie settled in the Lyons region with his young wife. Marcel and Eddie led the rest of their siblings to Marseilles. Yvette took an apartment near her elder brothers and ran a household which included her three daughters, Gilda, and her four stepbrothers and stepsisters, Claire, Claude, Benjamin, and Aimée. When I interviewed them in Marseilles, Marcel and Eddie were running a butcher shop together. Claude had opened his own butcher's shop after his marriage in 1968, and Benjamin, who was also married, worked in a butcher's shop in town after having spent some time working with his elder brothers. Yvette was the manager of the nursing department of Baumettes Prison, a job she had obtained as the widow of an employee of the prison administration in Algeria. In 1979 the Marseilles part of the sibling group kept up very close ties, meeting almost every day, working together, and living within a kilometre of each other. The first cousins of the second generation, the children of Eddie and Clarisse and of Yvette and Marcel and Rosette's adopted daughter, also often saw each other and went out together. The women, Yvette, Clarisse, and Rosette, would meet several times a week, particularly during religious holidays. Zahra Akoun, who had been widowed a few years earlier, lived very near her sister-in-law Clarisse. Little Mouna Akoun lived with her younger son and her two daughters, Irène and Denise, in the Paris area. She had retired, and her daughters had executive assistant positions in administrative companies. Her younger son ran a travel agency. It was Claude Senoussi, his childhood friend, who suggested that I get in touch with Guy Bakoushe, who was then living in a Paris suburb. The two friends still wrote to each other and visited each other from time to time during holidays. Their narratives are dominated by the themes of adolescence in a country at war, the death of their father, and the frantic pursuit of a career. Zahra Akoun's eldest son, Elie, a dentist and married, had remained rooted in the Judaeo-Maghrebian culture while following a religious path that his contemporaries had long since abandoned.

On the Muslim side, Bou-Slimo was working in a company canteen in Sétif. His eight children were all at school or studying at the university. His eldest daughter, Amina, was thirty and unmarried, teaching French in an elementary school. She lived at home with her parents, and her salary was the largest contribution to the family's budget. She was my main guide in the quasi-archaeological exploration of Dar-Refayil's memoirs. She often came with me when I visited the house and saw her old neighbours and friends there. All these people relived in memory the epic of a house rooted in time through its cultural foundations and through the permanent and powerful social ties it had created.

5

The poetics of remembrance

Resigning himself to the decline of Jewish memory, Yerushalmi argues nevertheless that 'hardly any Jew today is without some Jewish past' (1989:99). Although he apparently intends to examine the 'elementary structures of Jewish memory', following Halbwachs he actually approaches the Jews' relation to their past without consideration of the immediate conditions for its social production. Contemporary Jewish memory depends, in my view, on more contingent symbolic and social processes. The past of contemporary Jews has little in common with traditional literate Jewish memory, which uses the structures of biblical narrative to explain History. It is rarely interpreted through the filter of the religious matrix. It is also rarely *inscribed*; it seldom claims to be writing History and actually bears an ambiguous relation to it. The hermeneutics of the past is no longer exclusively religious in scope and in methodology, although to some extent it employs the structures of religious thought. The relation of the vast majority of contemporary Jews to their past is marked by the experiences of genocide or emigration, or both.

Recent works have examined this contingency of post-Auschwitz Jewish memories, searching for models very different to the ones that governed traditional memory. Historical research undertaken by Wievorka and Niborski (1983) and Kugelmass and Boyarin (1983) explores the structure of the memory of the Holocaust in the memorial books of Polish Jews. This memory is thus still literary in nature, and its analysis obviously belongs to the history of literate culture. The book is memory. From a different methodological perspective, that of traditional oral history, Valensi and Wachtel decipher the memories of Eastern European and Mediterranean Jews settled in France (Valensi 1986, Valensi and Wachtel 1991). Following in the footsteps of Yerushalmi, however, Valensi unravels in these memories the structures of religious thought through which most of the recent experiences of her interviewees, including those of the massive migrations of the 1960s, are interpreted. In the most recent work remembrance is collected and analysed in terms of its *narrative* structure; memory is seen as a narrative art[1] and interpreted as a text (Geertz 1973). Whereas for Yerushalmi the main question was whether the Jewish commandment of remembrance was supported by a genuine historiographic endeavour, what are now being examined are the symbolic structures and the logic of memorial narrative – how collectivities, more like poets than like historians, elaborate a textual treatment of their past. This approach can be observed in Lapierre's work on the memories of Plock's Jews (1989), Namer's on the social memory of Egyptian Jews living in France (1987:129–34), Pollak's on concentration camp survivors (1990), Benveniste's on Ladino speakers in Paris (1989), and Boyarin's on Polish Jews in Paris (1991). It is no longer the mere *social* dimension of memory that scholars explore but its narrative logic as well. Thus the most recent approaches to Jewish memory, inspired by hermeneutic anthropology, explore a cultural process based on a concept of time as 'reversible' (Lévi-Strauss 1963) that is similar to the construction of mythical narrative (Benveniste 1989:54).

The construction of remembrance in Dar-Refayil's memoirs has a similar symbolic logic. There is in what one might call domestic thought a certain 'poetics of space', a 'topo-analysis' (Bachelard 1969). Remembrance of the house evolves as a narrative interpretation of the past. The description of the house is articulated in terms of a combination of discursive signs from which can be read a social discourse. A similar logic operates in the property advertisements deciphered by Augé (1989): a semantic system is at work here, governed by a social rhetoric extending far beyond the realm of language (Herzfeld 1985). Thus this narrative procedure is more than a mere embellishment of the past, as some scholars have argued with regard to other social contexts (Valensi 1986, Valensi and Wachtel 1991). It also *manipulates* the past by investing it with meaning through the complex devices leading to the elaboration of a specific discursive genre.

The collective memory presented here is a significant example of dissemia (Herzfeld 1987:152). The ethnographic study of collective memory involves two levels of analysis corresponding to the two structural levels of memorial narrative: that of semiotic anthropology, which aims to unravel the mental processes whereby a group relates to its past through the formulation of collective memories, and that of ethnohistory, which assembles a corpus of data on a period of the group's history accounted for by collective remembrance. The preceding chapters have shuttled between these two levels – between reality as it has been lived and experienced and the lessons of oral history.

Memory, narrative, and identity

Dar-Refayil's memoirs were delivered to me as oral narratives and structured in terms of the social and cultural processes of narrative composition. According to several ethnographers of Jewish folklore, these oral narratives are an established tradition in a number of Jewish cultures (Kirshenblatt-Gimblett 1978,1989, Mintz 1968). Storytelling had long been part of the popular culture of Dar-Refayil's Jews, as my hosts indicated when they evoked the evenings they spent listening to their fathers' or mothers' stories. Their recollections of these reunions are a discourse on narrative, a narrative of narrative, a narrative moulded in another narrative. In some portions of memorial narratives a memory of a narrative emerges, although it is not made explicit: 'I remember that my mother told me that in her childhood she used to . . .' Some of the events mentioned in these recollections have not been directly experienced by their narrators, who had not been born yet or had come onto the scene only later. For example, Rosette tells about Sarah's death as if she had experienced it directly, whereas in fact she married Marcel twelve years afterward. Her story implies another story told to her by the group she had joined. Similarly, Moushi's oldest children talk about the origins of the Senoussis before their arrival in Sétif where they themselves were born. A number of memorial narratives are in fact second-hand versions of narratives already transmitted as such. Our narrators tell what they have been told or what they remember of what they have been told.

Dar-Refayil's memoirs recount a series of migrations and deracinations; they are a wandering narrative. They suggest an ancient tradition of storytelling used as a source of family identity. Young and old, parents and children, men and women all contributed to the process, stimulating each other's recollections. During one of my interviews with Clarisse, her daughter Viviane interrupted to supplement and stimulate her mother's narration: 'Have you told her what you used to call your eldest brother? . . . Tell her how you used to go to the farm on the last day of Passover . . . Have you told her about your excursions to the sulphur springs that you used as a spa? . . . Have you told her that you used to bake your own Passover bread?' One can perceive in this process the impact of the ancient practice of storytelling in the house and among North African Jews in general and its use as a model for the reconstruction of historical memory.[2]

In reproducing the story of the family's origins, narrators symbolically place themselves in the genealogical history for which the house constitutes the material background. Striking in this process, the frequent migrations are grounded in the stability of the house. Migrations and peregrinations are transfigured by the predominance of the spatial dimension of narrative development. Yet the image of the house is less meaningful than the verbal structure of the construction of memory. It is the word that creates the image and not the other way around. Dar-Refayil's memoirs show that without the verbal reconstruction of spatial images the connection with history, geography, and the uniqueness of Jewish destiny would be threatened.

Time subordinated to space

Recent work on the sociology, history, and ethnography of Jewish memory has paid little attention to the dialectic relation between the spatial construction of memory and the experience of migration. In the memories of Plock's Jews analysed by Lapierre (1989:81–109), the account of migrations is built on a vision of hasty time, a 'counted-out' time which ignores space, a time in which experiences unfold in motion without taking shape in particular places. Domestic space exists in this memory only through the nostalgic (and tragic) evocation of 'time lost': along with its former residents killed in Auschwitz, remembered domestic space disappears. Dar-Refayil's narratives have a different logic. In them the protagonists' migrations seem to start from the house and return to it. The house is the narrative's centripetal metaphor.

To remember, one has to build, or rebuild. Yates opened up this perspective with her work on the art of memory in ancient and medieval European thought (1966). Spence went further in this direction with his intellectual biography of Matteo Ricci, a sixteenth century Jesuit priest who undertook to educate the Chinese on the mnemotechnic procedures he had rediscovered through his reading of the ancient philosophers (1984). The crux of Yates's and Spence's argument is the power of the image in the construction of memory, this imagery being materialized in the representation of specific places and the people associated with them.

By the same logic, the imaginative dominance of domestic places in Dar-Refayil's memoirs is a discursive form of the subordination of time to immediate space or, rather, a fusion of time and space, giving to a quasi-cosmological dimension to the architecture of memory (Fabian 1983:111;

Casey 1987:214). It is through the evocation of the daily use of objects in the house that narrative develops a description of social life and economic conditions in Sétif. Remembered objects and places are made historiographers, sociologists of the past. Some of these objects, such as the kitchen utensils, have been brought along on the journey to France, but on the whole Dar-Refayil's former Jewish residents are not *physically* attached to the objects that surrounded them in their Setifian domestic life. Memory has stored them in its oral archives, as if their materiality could exist only in remembrance. Domestic space and objects are more important for their symbolic than for their practical function. This is so because the repetitiveness of their past use has inscribed them and the associated social exchanges in the cultural order. While being used they also were present in *thought* and transferred into the register of memory. Thus memory effects the shift from the practical to the symbolic.

In his analysis of the representation of the house among Kabyle peasants, Bourdieu writes, 'The meaning objectified in the objects or places of the space fully reveals itself only through practices according to the very schemas organized in relation to them (and reciprocally)' (1980:445, my translation). Memory is thus carried by a *habitus* (Bourdieu 1977a) of which it is the symbolic representation. Within uprooted memory, domestic space acts as a 'mute and motionless society' (Halbwachs 1980:129). Female and male places, private and collective space, corners for parents and children's nooks, places reserved for hygiene, sexualized places and culinary spaces, places for working and places for resting, all these oppositions within domestic space refer to the oppositions structuring social relations. Domestic space is an objectified social organization. Yet this concreteness is an illusion: it is in fact the material *representation* of the social order. Memory records it as such in retaining the symbolic structures inscribed in the domestic arrangement, transforming objects into semantic units. In this process, social reproduction is achieved through the symbolic perpetuation of the social order *represented* in the habitat. Behind the remembrance of each object is that of an experience shared with a neighbour, a relative, a cousin, a brother or sister. Remembering the original house is in fact recalling the social and cultural milieu in which one grew up, laughed, and cried. Remembrance of the original house is the representation of the epitome of the social order.

The subordination of time to space in Dar-Refayil's memoirs recalls Bakhtin's chronotope, which 'expresses the indissolubility of space and time . . . Time is here condensed, becomes compact, visible for art, while space is intensified, engulfed by the movement of time, the subject,

History. The signs of time are discovered in space, which is perceived and measured in terms of time' (1978:237, my translation). In Dar-Refayil's memoirs, time is not the rhythm of narrative; it is objectified in the materiality of domestic space.

This chronotope aspect of memory is a dominant narrative model in another Maghrebian cultural form, the Francophone novel. Thus in *La grande maison* Mohammed Dib (1952) dramatizes the poverty of prewar colonial Algeria by sealing it in the materiality of the domestic space. The story of Dar-Sbitar, a collective household similar to Dar-Refayil, is in fact the story of the Algerian people dominated and crushed by poverty. Here, too, the house is the material representation of a social destiny. This Maghrebian house is all the more meaningful in the communication of a collective experience because its architecture, on which the narrative semantic is constructed, carries images of plurality and conviviality. It is as if the entire Algerian people were represented in its courtyard. The house embodies what Bachelard calls an 'intimate immensity' (1969:183).

Autobiography: making the particular universal

The narrators' story opens and closes within this enclosed space. Their adventures are initiated in the house and in a sense entwine themselves around it. However, narratives also trace individual trajectories, daily exchanges between neighbours, the fate of families, friendships, and the position of Dar-Refayil's children within the Setifian community. Finally, they tell how remembrance has preserved the major upheavals of the late colonial period, the rise of Arab nationalism, the Second World War, the war of independence, and the great departure for France. On the one hand, Dar-Refayil's memoirs report on the past in a restricted place and the narrow life of its residents. They dwell on the smallness of this universe, so poorly equipped and uncomfortable, and on the rudimentary life people lived there. Yet the other side of the story emphasizes the plural and universal dimension of a domestic society in which diverse languages, cultures, religions, and family histories coexisted side by side. The tale of Dar-Refayil crosses the boundary between private and public, between the particular and the universal.[3]

The familial character of this tale gives it the shape of a collective destiny, but the story moves with the residents from their domestic experiences to their experiences in the city, as members of a plural urban community, and as members of the Jewish community. Women are secluded up to a certain point and then gradually go out for diversion after a silent struggle within the domestic world. When they finally reach the street, remembered experiences replicate there the relationships established in the house: friends from the inner world are met again outside. Finally, the Second World War and the war of independence cross the threshold of the house and infiltrate the intimate workings of domestic cohesion, constantly threatened and defended.

Between private and public, the courtyard occupies a special locus: a place of intimacy and also of ingathering; it is here that are celebrated the life-cycle rituals in which outsiders are invited into the domestic world. Thus, in addition to being centripetal to the narrative the house serves as the meeting of transition between private and public, between the particular fate of the domestic group and local and regional history. Although the main protagonists of the tale are the house's residents, the narratives also deal with the universal dimension of their experiences, inside and outside. Their autobiography is that of humankind writ small. While tracing the boundaries between the world of the self and that of the Other, it speaks in the first person but in fact addresses others.

However, this close link between the particular and the universal involves a dramatic point of tension, a sort of structural break. In a number of narratives the 'I' is replaced by 'we' or 'one'. In one way or another, narrators express their former feeling of having been smothered by a community now perceived as intrusive rather than protective. In order to succeed in their careers, to be able to start a family and look after it, everyone needs to leave the mother-house. This emerges as a major dilemma in most narratives. It is as if the structural and narrative logic of all the accounts were leading to the shattering of the domestic group and the conclusion of the domestic epic. As the narratives progress, the collective no longer appears idyllic and gradually evaporates. The migration to France constitutes the culmination of this gradual erasure of the house as a metaphor for collective security. The narrative that found its integrity within the unity of the domestic world concludes with its dislocation.

Negatives of the past

The semantic and discursive structure of this narrative lies in the status and identity of its producers and listeners and in the social conditions of its production. The Senoussi family is its principal producer and transmitter. It is Senoussi history that its members aim to rewrite, its past that they aim to re-create. The message contained in this discourse transforms the Senoussis into the bearers of a humanist ethic. It is, however, the women who take the lead in the transmission of this message. They were particularly cooperative in my investigations, providing abundant details even on very intimate matters, talking about what had been their realm, the place where they had spent most of their time, where they had tried to develop the power they did not enjoy elsewhere. Women do not idealize their past in Dar-Refayil. They often stress having been imprisoned in their daily life. At the same time, however, their narratives transform a dominated world into a haven of social cohesion. It is as if the word and remembrance had given voices to those who had not had them in the past that they were recounting. The effect of nostalgia is equivalent to a reversal of status. The main producers of Dar-Refayil's memoirs are those who could not speak in the past. Time has empowered them, and memory produces authority. The small become great and the weak mighty.

In this spirit, it is as uprooted people that the Senoussis report on their past and on their life when the family was united and sheltered within the house. They talk about a past just preceding the time when it all fell apart, when all the relatives were dispersed and the house lost most of its Jewish residents. The domestic community no longer exists; memory saves it from oblivion, legitimates it in history, eternalizes it. The process is not a new one in the relation of Jews to their past. Yerushalmi describes it as a structural pattern in the medieval Jewish art of memory (1989). Udovitch and Valensi analyse the discursive modes whereby Jews in Djerba legitimate their ancestral presence on the island through their founding narratives (1984). Auschwitz survivors' published memoirs were particularly abundant in the first few years after the Second World War, imprinting their recollections before they could sink into oblivion, before the horror could be obliterated (Pollak and Heinich 1986:13–14).

However, the narrative logic of Dar-Refayil's memoirs is very different from that of similar forms of memorial narratives in rural societies, even though the latter often aim to legitimate the rooting of a genealogical group in the territory (Assier-Andrieu 1987). Here the narrative goal is not challenged by any sort of competition for the legitimation of land tenure. What is at stake is the preservation of the *symbolic* heritage of a domestic group after migration and deracination. The house will no longer be visited by its former Jewish residents; they will no longer visit the graves of the relatives that inhabit their memories. There is an irreversible separation between those who remember and the object of their remembrance. The past urban landscape has completely disappeared from sensory experience. None of Dar-Refayil's former residents can (or want to) confront their memories with the present reality. None of them will ever see again the corner of the balcony where sabbath pots were lined up, the street corner where they played football with their friends from the neighbourhood, the tree in the courtyard. Memory has taken over the space left empty in sensory experience. It is a distant and intangible relation to the past. The past appears as a *negative* of the present. Remembrance has manufactured a 'negative of the house, the reverse of the function of inhabiting' (Bachelard 1969:42), employing a quasi-'photographic' process that consists in recovering a positive image from the 'negative' of the past. This is why narratives include such a wealth of memories of sensory experiences – of festivals that are seen, heard, and smelled. Physical estrangement from past places has crystallized the collective memory of the house. The remembrance of the original house is part of the syndrome of exile; it poeticizes an intimate and enclosed space that one can no longer touch. What is at work here is a narrative process of 'historical inversion' much like that of the folkloric chronotope (Bakhtin 1978:294). Similarly, Dar-Refayil's memoirs seek to invert the social and geographical order. Remembrance not only aims to *reflect* the past but also sublimates it. It presents itself as the negotiation or symbolic resolution of the conflicts arising from history and society.

The moral of history

As in myths of origin, memory tells how and why the group was formed, what constitutes its founding event, what determines its collective destiny. As do a number of myths of origin, Dar-Refayil's story begins with a tragedy and ends with a tragedy: it is circumscribed by death. At the beginning, a mother dies, and the family is shattered. Children wander from one aunt to the next; the heartbroken father decides to leave the funereal house and settle in Dar-Refayil. He remarries, and new children are born from this new marriage. Dar-Refayil's community continues to grow, new families arrive. Memory aims to convey the message of the strength of family values: a family is broken by a tragic abortion (a non-birth, a rupture in familial demography), but entry into the house is an act of salvation. The house is saviour, refuge; it restores the original family order. It is a new womb ready to be fertilized. The locus of memory becomes a woman's fertile body (Casey 1987:147).

In the end, families gradually leave the house to find better jobs in the city. Domestic harmony is disturbed by the war. The father's death concludes the epic. Dar-Refayil's story is told as a completed life cycle, that of a family, that of *the* family. Its hero is the family. It aims to convey at once the family's vulnerability and its stability. Memoirs are always written about completed experiences, giving them this appearance of a finished product, an accomplished fact. Dar-Refayil's story is presented as a relentless struggle against all sorts of dangers and tragedies, against the difficulty of earning a meagre living, preserving the family intact, and surviving the war. From this viewpoint, it is no mere embellishment of the past. To transform people and groups into heroes, narratives emphasize the harshness of their life and the severity of their fate and point to the way they managed to brave adversity (Valensi and Wachtel 1991). Apparent in this narrative scenario is the structure of what Bakhtin identifies as the 'novel as idyll' (1978:376) and, in particular, a novel which, evoking the family idyll, is built on the essential structure of kinship that relates the protagonists. Within this system, the characters' peregrinations tend to focus narrowly on the family dwelling which ensures the integrity of the narrative scenario. Similarly, in Dar-Refayil's memoirs the house stands not only as a symbol of past achievements but also as a model of the ideal past projected into the future. This is the process of 'historical inversion' discussed earlier.

The same process can also be found in the evocation of the theme of distinction and boundaries. The house is an enclosed world traversed by spatial, social, economic, and religious distinctions. There are doors and windows, some opening onto the interior and others to the exterior. Overcrowding is everywhere, encumbering the most intimate relationships. Memory clearly re-creates the sense of a separation made difficult by the layout of domestic space. But despite the cramped quarters there was 'respect' and conviviality between Jewish and Muslim neighbours, between men and women, and between families of different social status. Women called Dar-Refayil the 'Cour des Miracles' because of the mutual respect that made it possible to survive these conditions. In addition, in the house residents found the respect that they could not find outside, in colonial society. Respect was in a way a form of social control. During religious festivals, everyone was invited. Muslim women could not attend them, but they would still participate by donating food. Memory finds in the past house the respect that those who left it had failed to find in France. Constant contrasts between past respect and dignity and present selfish individualism are scattered throughout the narratives, as if the past aimed to instruct the present and carried aspirations for the future – as if a moral were being projected onto the past.

Memory in performance
Though narrative in nature and structure, this collective memory not only speaks but also is performed (Bauman 1977). As we have seen, the family reunion for festive celebrations is one of the most spectacular forms of

performed memory. What is characteristic of these performative processes is that they are diverse, multiple, and endlessly reinvented. One of the social and symbolic practices they cover is the system of objects, which has the advantage of giving a concrete shape to the connection with the past. There is no memory without objects, Halbwachs writes (1980). Images are the most powerful of these objects, both stimulating and channelling remembrance: photographs of places and people, deceased relatives, and life-cycle celebrations, with special emphasis on weddings.[4] This memory objectified in images was often displayed on the walls of the houses and the display participated in the 'socio-analysis' generated by my inquiry (Delsaut 1988).

The most stimulating image, however, was the one I requested myself, one that had apparently remained invisible and silent for many years but was nevertheless present in the mapping of memory – the plan of the house. It was presented as the engraving of remembrance, as a representation with all the characteristics of the real thing. 'An objective drawing of this kind', Bachelard writes, 'independent of all daydreaming, is a forceful, reliable document that leaves its mark on biography' (1969:49). When I visited the house in 1980, I used the plan drawn by my hosts to find their former Muslim neighbours and to locate everyone in the past universe described. My interlocutors had also used it as a guide for their memory in action.

Another performative structure is inscribed in the linguistic construction of memory. Here memorial language is conceived not simply as a mere lexical or syntactic system but also as a system of practices. The ethnography of remembrance is, as we have seen, an ethnography of intercultural speech. Although the principal language used in narratives is French, because it is the language used every day by my Jewish hosts, Arabic and Judaeo-Arabic emerge at intervals in narratives as languages of the past now abandoned. There is a narrative logic in the alternation of these languages: the code switching indicates a temporal shift. French is the language of the present (and of the future), Arabic that of the past and of backwardness. Thus women, in particular, point to these practices by having their protagonists speak Arabic, 'as in the old days'. Code-switching carries a historical meaning: it suggests the emancipation and Westernization of the Jews. The alternation of the two languages bridges two epochs; it is a discourse on modern history, an ethno-philosophy of history. In addition, the shift from French to Arabic is a memorial communication between the narrators and their protagonists, most often deceased relatives. Narrators and their protagonists speak two different languages. Thus memory is here a process of *translating* communication with the past – translating the past rather than re-creating it.

Memories of practices and the practice of memory

Remembrance of Dar-Refayil is sealed in the concreteness of material life. The most vivid memories are those evoking quotidian exchanges, gestures, and words unfolding within this space. For the former Muslim residents, remembering their Jewish neighbours essentially consists in mentioning their religious festivals, their ritual foods, and the Judaeo-Muslim exchanges which took place on these occasions. They remember Gilda falling asleep on her low stool after an evening chat, children tasting hot bread just baked, the Sunday meetings over laundry which gathered Jewish women in the courtyard. Domestic memory focuses not only on images of *places* but also on images of *concrete acts*. Its key dimensions are action, concreteness, and immediacy. People remember *doing* things. Remembrance of socialized domestic space is thus based above all on the *practice* of this space as it is articulated in the repeated interactions of its agents.[5] Remembrance of the house is the symbolic locus for the *embodiment* of social practices experienced in daily life; it constitutes a system of 'bodily practices' (Casey 1987, Connerton 1989).

It may seem paradoxical that this practical dimension of domestic space inhabited physically in the past and through memory in the present has entered the symbolic register with the experience of deracination. Past practices have been aggregated into a symbolics of practice as if the temporal distance from the past and the geographical estrangement of an uprooted group had effected the merging of the practical and the symbolic. The practices are all the more symbolic in that they have ceased to occur and the group that elaborated them is estranged from the space in which they unfolded. From this viewpoint, uprooted memory anchors the symbolic in the practical and generates the symbolizing of past practices. This merging of symbolic and practical shows that memory establishes an operative link between the practice of the social order and its symbolic representation.[6]

Notes

Introduction: the ethnologist and her double

1. During this expedition to the *hammam*, the presence of my friend Fanny Mergui, a psychotherapist born in Morocco, helped to stimulate remembrance of the Maghrebian past. She had accompanied me on my exploratory trip to Marseilles during the spring vacation, and our conversations about it stimulated my thinking. I thank her for her emotional and intellectual support.

2. In fact, I ended up adopting the common practice in anthropological writing of changing the names of persons and the house itself to protect my informants' privacy.

3. This ethnographic position has been addressed in several recent works, such as Ruth Behar's *Translated Woman* (1993). In my own case, 'dictation' seems more apt than 'translation', since my informants are integrated into the culture of the 'Other' and have already proceeded to the translation of their culture by migration and assimilation.

4. This academic legitimation can be found in particular in Cohen (1912), Desparmet (1939), Bahloul (1983), Friedman (1988), and Valensi and Wachtel (1991).

5. See earlier analyses of this epistemological question by Fabian (1983), Herzfeld (1987), Clifford and Marcus (1986), and Behar (1993).

1 Foundations

1. The Alliance Israélite Universelle was an international network of schools set up in the nineteenth century by prominent French Jews. Its aim was to make it possible for the Jews in the Middle East and Eastern Europe to achieve social and economic emancipation by giving their children access to secular education (Rodrigue 1989).

2. Although this percentage is lower than it was in the last years of the nineteenth century, the Jewish population did increase in the first two decades of the twentieth century, though less than the general population.

3. Rabbi Maurice Eisenbeth originally came from Alsace, where he had received

his rabbinical training, and was chief rabbi in Algeria until the 1950s. He devoted himself to the history and sociology of his Algerian coreligionists and published a number of articles and several books on the subject. Though often biased by his position in the local community, his work nevertheless remains a precious source of information on the Algerian Jewish societies of his time (Eisenbeth 1945).

4. In other areas of the Mediterranean basin, this building type shelters extended families, patriarchal or patrilineal, usually consisting of parents, their married male children's households, and other unmarried or widowed kinsmen (Al-Messiri Nadim 1979, Boudjedra 1971, Brandes 1975, 1980 and 1990, Côte 1988, Desparmet 1939, Davis 1977, Eickelman 1980, Maunier 1930, Pitkin 1985 and 1990, Udovitch and Valensi 1984).

5. *Oustal* means 'house' in Langue d'Oc (spoken in Southwestern France). *Oustal* 'refers to a farm in the sense of a conjunction between a specific named place and the family line associated with it' (Rogers 1991: 68). In their work in rural Colombia, Gudeman and Rivera found a similar structuring of social life and economy on the model of the house. They contend that the house as a metaphor is an ancient Mediterranean institution imported to Latin America by Spanish colonization (1990:11).

6. This festival is celebrated twelve days after Yom Kippur, on the twenty-second day of the Hebrew calendar.

7. The French term used here is *évolué*, which actually denotes an advanced degree of cultural Westernization. During the final days of the colonial period, those adoptive 'French' who wanted to become integrated into European society used this term to contrast the socially elevated with the *arriéré* (backward), who were 'un-Westernized' and therefore on the lowest rungs of the colonial social ladder. One recognizes in this terminology the social evolutionism which was deeply entrenched in colonialist ideology in Algeria.

8. Female narrators used the French *trafiquée*, derived from the terminology of clandestine trade, thus suggesting the existence of an underground network using illicit and makeshift tools. The language used here is designed to signify how desperate young women aspiring to social advancement were in their bodily struggle with hermetic family structures.

9. See Emily Martin's (1987) analysis of the symbolic construction of reproduction in contemporary women's narrated lives.

10. By contrast, American working-class women express disapproval of abortion in a different historical and social context (Martin 1987:105). It is clear that attitudes towards abortion are governed not solely by class but by a complex set of sociocultural and historical strategies – indeed, by habitus (Bourdieu 1977a) – as Ginsburg (1989) has noted among activists in the American abortion debate.

11. This ideological process is reminiscent of the structures of the abortion debate in the late twentieth-century United States (Ginsburg 1989). Ginsburg points out that abortion activists' narratives display 'an apparent dissonance between cultural codes, social process, and individual transformation in the life course' (1987).

12. The sororate (whereby a widower marries his dead wife's sister) is a female form of the levirate (Deuteronomy 25:25) which allowed the household to

keep the goods and services that made up the dowry instead of returning them to the deceased's family; when the second spouse was one of the deceased's relatives, these goods were guaranteed to stay within the boundaries of the immediate kin group. The levirate aimed at avoiding the scattering and division of a family's wealth and preserving its emotional stability. It was not regulated by Jewish law but seems to have been quite common among Mediterranean Jews from early times (Goitein 1978:211).

13. The French term here is *petite cousine* ('little cousin'), which designates any cousin more distant than the first. Here the metaphor of size is applied to the classification of the kin group through the criterion of kinship *degree*. The opposite ('big cousin') was not, however, used to designate a first cousin.

14. At thirty-two, Gilda was considered a spinster, and her matrimonial value was low except in this case, by virtue of her being a relative of Moushi's. Her adoption by a maternal aunt was common among Jews in North Africa. Her sister had had the same experience, and there are similar adoptions in the subsequent generations. In the case of adoption, as in that of the sororate, the family provides fertile ground for the discovery of solutions to demographic tragedies. This was often the recourse chosen in the event of infertility, a problem which, because the women were generally blamed, was solved within the circle of female relatives.

15. As Ginsburg (1987) has observed among US pro-choice activists, abortion may be interpreted as an expression of one's commitment to family stability. For Sarah, aborting her sixth child had meant ensuring her other children's well-being and education. In the end, however, her death put an end to their education and to the family's upward mobility.

16. This pogrom was the culmination of a municipal election campaign which unfolded within the strongly anti-Jewish atmosphere typical of interwar politics in Algeria. On the other side of the political scene was a mood of incipient rebellion amongst the colonized Arab population. The French army cleverly exploited the vulnerability of the Jewish community, caught between two antagonistic trends, to deter Jews from playing an active part in the electoral race and then to divert attention towards a scapegoat. This pogrom played out a scenario characteristic of anti-Jewish uprisings in the Maghreb since the early twentieth century. A rumour was spread, with the help of the French military, about a Jew's having insulted the Muslim faithful near the mosque. (Some said that he had urinated on the building.) Tension grew in the Muslim population, and on the next day, 5 August 1934, there was a demonstration that rapidly developed into a riot. Jewish homes and shops were attacked and ransacked, and twenty-five people were slaughtered. The official reports of the Alliance Israélite Universelle (I.C.1) unambiguously describe the military inaction during the event; the French army did not intervene to stop the massacre. In fact, the gradual integration of Jews into local politics had generated resentment among the Arabs crushed under the colonial yoke and had thwarted the local French politicians' agendas (Abitbol 1990, Ageron 1979).

17. The term 'indigenous' was characteristic of the colonial classification of the populations inhabiting the French colonies of Africa. In Algeria it designated mainly the non-European communities. The Jews were included in this cate-

gory until they were granted French citizenship in 1870 and their deep integration into the school system in the decades thereafter. In the 1950s the term 'indigenous' denoted only the Muslim groups, Arab and Berber.

18. The 'subject' status referred to here is that of *dhimmis,* imposed by the Muslims on all non-Muslim communities (in Algeria mainly Jews and Christians) since the Arab conquest. This status of dependence and subjugation was abolished in Algeria with French colonization. The events of 1935 were reported by one of the administrators of the Alliance Israélite Universelle in Algeria in a letter addressed to the headquarters in Paris (I.C.1).

19. Most narratives, both Jewish and Muslim, mention El-'Ayyashi as a self-made dentist with no professional diploma who in fact mainly extracted teeth. The professional term is thus used as a term of endearment and a mocking pun.

20. One woman's narrative referred to the house as a 'Cour des Miracles' (a dirty, crowded place), borrowing Victor Hugo's trope from *Les Misérables.*

2 Telling places: the house as social architecture

1. Similar symbolic procedures have been reported in other Mediterranean societies (see Brandes 1980 and 1990; Eickelman 1980; and Hirschon 1978:76–77).

2. This is another significant similarity with the Greek domestic world (Hirschon 1978:76 and 77).

3. I am indebted to Marshall Leaffer for having suggested this analogy.

4. The term used by my interlocutors is the French *cagibi,* which designates a tiny, windowless area, generally located in a waste space beneath a stairway or at the bottom of a room.

5. In her narrative construction, Aimée's wandering bed generates the grammatical wandering of the subject: her account shifts from 'you' to 'one' and ends, almost timidly, with 'I'. Here the structural shift goes from the universal to the particular, a narrative shift which is quite common in the autobiographical genre (Joutard 1983, Myerhoff 1979).

6. Rosette's account of life in Dar-Refayil was what I would characterize as the most 'feminist' of all the female narratives. It was she who most strongly emphasized the lack of privacy and the crowding as a material form of control over women in the house. This is probably why she describes sexual activity in this sequence as being orchestrated by men: '*Eddie* made love . . .' Her narrative characterizes lack of privacy as a male – thus oppressive – register as opposed to the suggested female privacy and conviviality expressed in her mocking account.

7. The French word used in narratives is *toilettes à la turque,* referring to the long Ottoman occupation of Algeria until the modern period. In the fifties the phrase referred to an Oriental lifestyle viewed as archaic and radically opposed to the so-called evolved European one.

8. A few lucky women did get their own washing machines towards the end of the fifties.

9. These were part of the bride's trousseau and remained her property until her daughters' weddings.

10. This dish, made up of fat meats, vegetables, legumes, and grains, was cooked from nightfall on Friday to lunchtime on Saturday. It was the practical expression of the obligation to keep the fire constantly lit throughout the sabbath's twenty-four hours (Bahloul 1983).

11. The term 'symbolic' is used in this context in its common sense, 'not real'.

12. This aspect of domestic symbolism is found in other Mediterranean societies (Hirschon 1978 and 1989; Eickelman 1980).

13. Salt was bought in blocks and had to be crushed before use.

14. The Arabic term *'ers* literally means 'wedding (party)' or 'matrimonial atmosphere'. Giving *'ers* to the tree thus means dressing it up as if for a celebration.

15. A similar characteristic exists in Italian society (Pitkin 1985 and 1990).

16. However, they had had a special status on all fronts during the Second World War and had for the most part been confined to work camps (Abitbol 1990).

17. The term 'Catholic' is here used to designate Christian Europeans. There was a small Protestant community in Sétif, but the overwhelming majority of the Christian population was Catholic.

3 Telling people: the house and the world

1. The celebration of the bat mitzvah (the female equivalent) was not common in Sétif at the time.

2. Smoking on the sabbath is prohibited by Jewish law.

3. The name René (French for 'reborn') was often given to the first male child in the postwar period. It figured in Jewish popular culture as the translation of the Hebrew name Hayim, which means 'life'. Thus it signified the rebirth of the patriline, a particular godsend if the boy was the firstborn (see details in Bahloul 1985a).

4. Here Clarisse unambiguously locates patrilineal reproduction in the sacred register.

5. Even when sons set up their own households, it was never very far from their father's house – in the same street, the same neighbourhood, sometimes even the same building.

6. Guy uses here the translation of the Hebrew holiday Shavuoth, which was often referred to by Algerian Jews in terms of its correspondence with Christian ritual of Pentecost.

7. She herself wore the traditional Jewish dress, slightly different from the Muslim one.

8. Elie Akoun and his brothers and Little Mouna's children were the only ones to be educated beyond the high-school level. Among them today are a dentist, a certified accountant, two executive assistants, and a few middle managers.

9. In his critique of Greek ethnography, Herzfeld points out that this symbolic appropriation of domestic power by women is a Mediterranean reality that often contradicts the Western cliché of oppressed Southern European women (1991a and 1991b). Rogers reached a similar conclusion in her analysis of gender relations in Southwestern French peasant society (1975 and 1991).

10. This wavering manifested itself in my own rapport with my female hosts. When I showed some of them a first draft of this manuscript, they criticized it

for overemphasizing the patriarchal structure of the domestic community: 'Women ruled Dar-Refayil, not men!'

11. In the first half of the twentieth century Jewish families most commonly adopted young girls. Adopters were childless couples or parents with no male children. In this family-oriented society, childlessness was perceived as a personal and collective disaster and was blamed at the outset on female sterility. In almost all cases the adoption took place within the consanguinal group and preferably the uterine kin group. A woman who had been fortunate enough to give birth to a large progeny would agree to give up one of her children to her childless sister, especially if she did not have the means to feed and raise the child properly. Girls were preferably the ones given away (I never came across a case of a boy being adopted through this system), since boys were too precious as genealogical elements in the agnatic structure. Adoption was carried out without recourse to secular law and very rarely endorsed by a court decision. It was guaranteed only by family logic and recognition.

12. The narrator does not specify the exact degree of kinship when mentioning this cousin. The rhetoric of memory presents this form of endogamy as evidence of resistance to Westernization, especially as regards women's status. It is thus sufficient for the narrator to indicate that her future spouse was a consanguinal relative, a concept generically designated by the term 'cousin'. In fact, in most terms of kinship address and classification among North African Jews, the category 'cousin' actually denotes a 'relative' in the general sense (see Bahloul 1985b and 1992a).

13. Rosette here uses the 'Christian' translation of bar mitzvah.

14. Closed doors are here opposed to the ever-open doors of Dar-Refayil as clear evidence of the lower status of the collective house's residents.

15. In families known to provide substantial financial means to their daughters, a ritual called *qowem*, consisting of a public display of the trousseau, was performed a few days prior to the wedding. The bride's female relatives would present the trousseau to the groom's family in front of a rabbi, who would record its components. This ritual was not performed in Dar-Refayil: its endogamy made it unnecessary to provide guarantees of the spouses' social positions.

16. Although Jews and Muslims share a prohibition on the consumption of pork, the Muslim religious code allows certain food items and combinations that are strictly excluded from the Jewish diet, among other things most shellfish and subterranean animals and the culinary association of milk and meat.

17. Similar processes were at work in the Jewish community of Batna (Friedman 1988:40, 63–64, 79, 80).

18. The Mozabites were another Berber group, mainly active in the food trade. Colonial ideology assigned them the pejorative label *moutchou*.

19. This term, borrowed from the Spanish *mujer* ('woman'), acquired a very pejorative connotation in colonial times.

20. The French word *colon* (here translated 'colonist') designated a farmer of European descent who possessed land on which Muslim workers were employed. Very few Jews occupied this socioeconomic position in colonial Sétif, and those who did were among the wealthiest.

21. The summer ritual celebrating the Pentateuch, the Torah, seven weeks after the first day of Passover.
22. This translation strategy could also be found in most Algerian Jewish communities during this period (Friedman 1988).
23. He means the past subjunctive, a grammatical form used mainly by upper-class speakers. In colonial Sétif, this form functioned socially as what Bourdieu calls an 'incorporated grammar' (1982:52).
24. The similarity of this nickname to 'SS', which in French refers to the Nazis, suggests a linguistic analogy between French colonial rule and the German occupation.
25. Herzfeld analyses this process in the modern Eastern Mediterranean context as one of the major assets of the Western ideological representation of the Greek world (1987:111).
26. Arab women and men displayed a similar trend a generation later.
27. A similar semantic is used in Greek by the urban communities of Piraeus. Hirschon (1978:77) reports that according to her informants one of the unpleasant effects of witchcraft was the 'tying down' of its victims.
28. This type of pilgrimage was practised in other Jewish communities of the Maghreb which had more strikingly saintly figures. These pilgrimages gave rise to frequent ritual interactions between Jews and Muslims (Ben-Ami 1981:283; Dermenghem 1954).
29. I am grateful to Jacques Hassoun for drawing my attention to this hypothesis.

4 Domestic time

1. This system of restrictions consists in the prohibition of consumption of leavened products such as bread and pastries, beer, and some cheeses (Bahloul 1983).
2. This is the ritual consisting in eliminating all residues of fermented foodstuffs from the household. It concludes the absolute purification that is required before the celebration of Passover.
3. The repetition of the man's geographical origin refers to the local customs that govern ritual menus.
4 Here Guy uses the Hebrew name of the festival meaningfully to characterize the religious dimensions of ethnic boundaries in Sétif.
5. Clarisse in fact uses the term *galette*, a flat bread.
6. The ritual frying recalls the oil of the lamps of the Jerusalem temple, which remained lit for a full week after Greek soldiers had profaned the premises. In fact, Jewish Setifian households commemorated the 'miracle' of the lamps by keeping hot oil on the stoves for a full week. In addition, they lit a candle each day on the special candelabra called the *hanukiya*.
7. This ritual consisted of a gathering of women who checked whether the nuptial sheets had been bloodstained; it was still practised in Sétif after the Second World War and sometimes jeopardized an engagement.
8. The use of the phrase 'anti-Jewish' rather than 'anti-Semitic' reflects the fact that the notion of anti-Semitism as a specific ideological system was not yet established in public opinion at the time.
9. As a form of recognition of the American liberators, numerous Maghrebian

Jewish families gave English first names to their children born at the end of the war or just after it (Bahloul 1985a).

10. There is, however, a major difference between Jewish and Muslim accounts. On the Muslim side, the episode has been remembered as an event emblematic of the Algerian struggle for national independence. The founding myth of the Algerian state is based on the Sétif riots. The Jewish uprooted memory operates with a different logic: the Jews have not forgotten May 1945, but for them it was not a major event in their irreversible trajectory towards France and the West.

11. This representation is also found in the Francophone Maghrebian literature of the postwar period (Dib 1952).

5 The poetics of remembrance

1. These works are partly inspired by both Bakhtin's contribution to the theory of narrative (1978, 1984) and Yates's approach to the art of memory (1966).

2. A similar process is analyzed by Kirshenblatt-Gimblett (1978:17), who describes the 'narrative creativity' with which immigrants reinterpret their experiences to transmit their values to their children.

3. This shift from public to private is examined by Pollak and Heinich (1986:13) in the memory of former deportees. Their narratives deny the individual and private dimension of the experience in concentration camps in favour of its universe.

4. Le Wita has used this procedure as an ethnographic device in her study of bourgeois family memory in France (1988).

5. By 'practice' I mean the constant composition and recomposition of an *experienced* space – its invention, its social making by its agents, who actively *inhabit* it rather than occupying fixed and preestablished structures (Bourdieu 1977a).

6. I refer here to the theories developed by Bourdieu (1980:7–41) and Fabre (1989).

Bibliography

Abitbol, Michel, 1990, *The Jews of North Africa During the Second World War*, Detroit: Wayne State University Press.

Abu-Lughod, Lila, 1993, *Writing Women's Worlds: Bedouin Stories*, Berkeley: University of California Press.

Ageron, Charles-Robert, 1979, *Histoire de l'Algérie contemporaine*, Paris: Presses Universitaires de France.

Alliance Israélite Universelle, Archives, Algérie.

Al-Messiri Nadim, Nawal, 1979, 'The Concept of the Hara: A Historical and Sociological Study of Al-Sukkariyya', *Annales Islamologiques*, 15, pp. 314–48.

Altorki, S., and Fawzi-El-Solh, C. (eds.), 1988, *Arab Women in the Field: Studying Your Own Society*, New York: Syracuse University Press.

Ardener, Shirley (ed.), 1981, *Women and Space: Ground Rules and Social Maps*, New York: St Martin's Press.

Assier-Andrieu, Louis, 1987, 'Maison de mémoire: structure symbolique du temps familial en Languedoc, Cucurnis', in *Terrain*, 9, pp. 10–33.

Augé, Marc, 1989, *Domaines et châteaux*, Paris: Seuil.

Aymard, Maurice, 1977, 'Espaces', in *La Méditerranée, l'espace et l'histoire*, ed. F. Braudel, pp. 191–223, Paris: Flammarion.

Ayoun, Richard, and Bernard Cohen, 1982, *Les Juifs d'Algérie: deux mille ans d'histoire*, Paris: J. C. Lattès.

Bachelard, Gaston, 1969, *The Poetics of Space*, trans. M. Jolas, Boston: Beacon Press. (First published in French, 1957.)

Bahloul, Joëlle, 1983, *Le culte de la Table Dressée*, Paris: Editions A.-M. Métailié.

1985a, 'Noms et prénoms juifs nord-africains', in *Terrain*, 4, pp. 62–9.

1985b, 'Stratégies familiales et reproduction socio-culturelle: parentèles juives nord-africaines en France', *Pardès*, 1(1), pp. 31–61.

1987, 'Les barrières coloniales,' in *Les Juifs d'Algérie: images et textes*, pp. 24–5, Paris: Editions du Scribe.

1992a, 'La famille sépharade dans la diaspora du XXème siècle', in *La société juive à travers l'histoire*, ed. Sh. Trigano, pp. 469–95, Paris: Fayard.

1992b, *La maison de mémoire*, Paris: Editions A.-M. Métailié.

Bakhtin, Mikhaïl, 1970, *L'oeuvre de François Rabelais et la culture populaire au Moyen Age*, Paris: Gallimard.

1978, *Esthétique et théorie du roman*, Paris: Gallimard.

1984, *Esthétique de la création verbale*, Paris: Gallimard.

Balfet, H., C. Bromberger, and G. Ravis-Giordani, 1976, *Pratiques et représentations de l'espace dans les communautés méditerranéennes*, Paris: Editions du CNRS.

Barth, Frederik, 1969, *Ethnic Groups and Boundaries*, Boston: Little, Brown.

Barthes, Roland, 1980, *New Critical Essays*, trans. R. Howard, New York: Hill and Wang.

Bauman, R. (ed.), 1977, *Verbal Art as Performance*, Rowley, Mass.: Newbury House.

Bauman, R., and J. Sherzer (eds.), 1989, *Explorations in the Ethnography of Speaking*, 2nd ed, Cambridge and New York: Cambridge University Press.

Bedoucha, G., 1980, 'La mémoire et l'oubli: l'enjeu du nom dans une société oasienne', *Annales, E.S.C.*, May–August, pp. 730–47.

1987, *L'eau, l'amie du puissant. Une communauté oasienne du Sud Tunisien*, Paris: Editions des Archives Contemporaines.

Behar, Ruth, 1993, *Translated Woman: Crossing the Border with Esperanza's Story*, Boston: Beacon Press.

Bel-Ange, Norbert, 1990, *Les Juifs de Mostaganem*, Paris: L'Harmattan.

Ben-Ami, I., 1981, 'The Folk Veneration of Saints among Moroccan Jews: Traditions, Continuity, and Change', in *Studies in Judaism and Islam*, ed. S. Morag, I. Ben-Ami, and N. Stillman, pp. 283–345, Jerusalem: Magnes Press.

Bensimon-Donath, Doris, 1962, *L'évolution de la femme israélite à Fès*, Travaux et Mémoires, no. 25, Aix-en-Provence: La Pensée Universitaire.

Benveniste, Annie, 1989, *Le Bosphore à la Roquette: la communauté judéo-espagnole à Paris (1914–1940)*, Paris: L'Harmattan.

Bergson, Henri, 1985 (1939), *Matière et mémoire, essai sur la relation du corps à l'esprit*, Paris: Presses Universitaires de France.

Bertaux-Wiame, Isabelle, 1988, 'Des formes et usages des histoires de famille', *L'Homme et la Société*, 90, pp. 25–35.

Bilu, Yoram, 1987, 'Dreams and the Wishes of the Saint', in *Judaism Viewed from Within and from Without: Anthropological Studies*, ed. H. Goldberg, pp. 285–313, Albany: State University of New York Press.

Boudjedra, Rachid, 1969, *La répudiation*, Paris: Denoël.

1971, *La vie quotidienne en Algérie*, Paris: Hachette.

Boudot, 1962, 'Du bled à la ville: l'exode intérieur des populations juives d'Algérie', *L'Arche*, 63, pp. 34–7.

Bourdieu, Pierre, 1963, *Sociologie de l'Algérie*, Paris: Presses Universitaires de France.

1977a, *Outline of a Theory of Practice*, New York and Cambridge: Cambridge University Press.

1977b, 'Le pouvoir symbolique', *Annales E.S.C.*, 32 (3), pp. 405–11.

1980, *Le sens pratique*, Paris: Editions de Minuit.

1982, *Ce que parler veut dire*, Paris: Fayard.

1986, 'L'illusion biographique', *Actes de la Recherche en Sciences Sociales*, 62–3, pp. 69–72.

1987, 'Fieldwork in Philosophy', in *Choses dites*, pp. 13–46, Paris: Editions de Minuit.

Boyarin, Jonathan, 1991, *Polish Jews in Paris: The Ethnography of Memory*, Bloomington: Indiana University Press.

Brandes, Stanley H., 1975, *Migration, Kinship, and Community: Tradition and Transition in a Spanish Village*, New York: Academic Press.

1980, *Metaphors of Masculinity: Sex and Status in Andalusian Folklore*, Philadelphia: University of Pennsylvania Press.

1990, 'Spanish Spatial Boundaries: Social Control and the State,' paper presented at the 89th annual meeting of the American Anthropological Association, New Orleans, November 27–December 2.

Bromberger, Christian, 1987, 'Du grand au petit. Variations des échelles et des objets d'analyse dans l'histoire récente de l'ethnologie de la France', in *Ethnologies en miroir: la France et les pays de langue allemande*, ed. I. Chiva, and U. Jeggle, pp. 67–94, Paris: Editions de la Maison des Sciences de l'Homme.

Bugeja, Marie, 1928–9, 'Les Juifs de la Kabylie', in *Bulletin de la Société de Conférences Juives d'Alger*, 3, pp. 101–25.

Camborieux, Armand, 1978, *Sétif et sa région*, Carcassonne: Imprimerie Gabelle.

Casey, Edward S., 1987, *Remembering: A Phenomenological Study*, Bloomington: Indiana University Press.

Chetrit, Joseph, 1980, 'Niveaux, registres de langue et sociolectes dans les langues judéo-arabes du Maroc', in *Les relations entre juifs et musulmans en Afrique du Nord: actes du colloque de Sénanque de 1978*, pp. 129–42, Paris: Editions du CNRS.

Chiva, I., 1987, 'La maison: le noyau du fruit, l'arbre, l'avenir', *Terrain*, 9, pp. 5–9.

Chiva, I., and U. Jeggle (eds.), 1987, *Ethnologies en miroir: la France et les pays de langue allemande*, Paris: Editions de la Maison des Sciences de l'Homme.

Clifford, James, 1985, 'De l'ethnographie comme fiction: Conrad et Malinowski', *Etudes Rurales*, nos. 97–8, pp. 47–67.

Clifford, James, and George E. Marcus (eds.), 1986, *Writing Culture: The Poetics of Ethnography*, Berkeley: University of California Press.

Cohen, Marcel, 1912, *Le parler arabe des Juifs d'Alger*, Paris: Champion.

Collomp, Alain, 1978, 'Maison, manières d'habiter et famille en Haute-Provence aux XVIIème et XVIIIème siècles', in *Ethnologie Française*, 4, pp. 301–20.

Connerton, Paul, 1989, *How Societies Remember*, Cambridge and New York: Cambridge University Press.

Côte, Marc, 1988, *L'Algérie ou l'espace retourné*, Paris: Flammarion.

Crapanzano, Vincent, 1977a, 'The Life History in Anthropological Field Work', *Anthropology and Humanism Quarterly*, 2, pp. 3–7.

1977b, 'On the Writing of Ethnography', *Dialectical Anthropology*, 2 (1), pp. 69–73.

1980, *Tuhami: Portrait of a Moroccan*, Chicago: University of Chicago Press.

Dakhlia, Jocelyne, 1990, *L'oubli de la cité: la mémoire collective à l'épreuve du lignage dans le jérid tunisien*, Paris: Editions La Découverte.

Davis, J., 1977, *People of the Mediterranean. An Essay in Comparative Social Anthropology*, London: Routledge and Kegan Paul.

de Certeau, Michel, 1984, *The Practice of Everyday Life*, Berkeley: University of California Press.

Delsaut, Yvette, 1988, 'Carnets de socioanalyse', 1, L'inforjetable; 2, Une photo de classe', *Actes de la Recherche en Sciences Sociales*, 74, pp. 83–6; 75, pp. 83–96.

La Dépêche de Constantine, since 1956 *La Dépêche de Constantine et de l'Est Algérien*.

Dermenghem, Emile, 1954, *Le culte des saints dans l'Islam maghrébin*, Paris: Gallimard.

Dermenjian, Geneviève, 1983, *Juifs et Européens d'Algérie: l'antisémitisme oranais, 1892–1905*, Jerusalem: Institut Ben-Zvi, Université Hébraïque.

Desparmet, Joseph, 1939, *Coutumes, institutions et croyances des indigènes de l'Algérie*, Vol. 1, Algiers: Imprimerie J. Carbonnel.

Dib, Mohammed, 1952, *La grande maison*, Paris: Seuil.

1957, *Le métier à tisser*, Paris: Seuil.

1985, *Les terrasses d'Orsol*, Paris: Sindbad.

Douglas, Mary, 1966, *Purity and Danger: An Analysis of Concepts of Pollution and Taboo*, London: Routledge and Kegan Paul.

Dubouloz-Laffin, Marie-Louise, 1933–4, 'Contribution à l'étude des jnoun et des divers états de possession dans la région de Sfax', *Revue Tunisienne*, 1933, pp. 321–49; 1934, pp. 227–66.

Duby, Georges, 1986, 'Le lignage', in *Les lieux de mémoire*, ed. Pierre Nora, vol. 2, pp. 31–56, Paris: Gallimard.

Dwyer, Kevin, 1977, 'On the Dialogic of Fieldwork', *Dialectical Anthropology*, 2 (2), 143–51.

1979, 'The Dialogic of Ethnology', *Dialectical Anthropology*, 4 (3), pp. 205–24.

1982, *Moroccan Dialogues: Anthropology in Question*, Baltimore: Johns Hopkins University Press.

Eickelman, Dale, 1980, 'Formes symboliques et espace social urbain,' in *Système urbain et développement au Maghreb*, pp. 199–218, Tunis: Cérès.

1989, *The Middle East, An Anthropological Approach*, 2nd edn, Englewood Cliffs, N.J.: Prentice Hall.

Eisenbeth, Maurice, 1931, *Le judaïsme nord-africain. Etudes démographiques sur les Israélites du département de Constantine*, Paris: Editions A. Natanson.

1934, 'Après les troubles de Constantine', *Univers Israélite*, 89 (51), pp. 706–8.

1936, *Les Juifs de l'Afrique du Nord: démographie et onomastique*, Algiers.

1945, *Pages vécues*, Algiers: Imprimerie Charras.

Encyclopedia Judaica, 1971, *s.v.* 'Algeria', 'Algiers', 'Bahutsim', 'Geneology', 'Levirate', Jerusalem: Keter.

L'Eveil de Sétif.

Fabian, Johannes, 1983, *Time and the Other: How Anthropology Makes Its Object*, New York: Columbia University Press.

Fabre, Daniel, 1989, 'Le symbolisme en question', in *L'autre et le semblable*, ed. Martine Segalen, pp. 61–78, Paris: CNRS.

Fanon, Frantz, 1952, *Peau noire, masques blancs*, Paris: Seuil.

Fischer, Michael, 1986, 'Ethnicity and the Post-Modern Arts of Memory', in

Writing Culture, ed. J. Clifford, and G. Marcus, pp. 194–233, Berkeley: University of California Press.

Foucault, Michel, 1981, *L'ordre du discours*, Paris: Gallimard.

Fremont, A., 1976, *La région, espace vécu*, Paris: Presses Universitaires de France.

Friedman, Elizabeth, 1988, *Colonialism and After: An Algerian Jewish Community*, South Hadley, Mass.: Bergin and Garvey.

Geertz, Clifford, 1973, *The Interpretation of Cultures*, New York: Basic Books.

1988, *Works and Lives: The Anthropologist as Author*, Stanford: Stanford University Press.

Geertz, Hildred, 1979, 'The Meaning of Family Ties,' in *Meaning and Order in Moroccan Society*, ed. C. Geertz, H. Geertz, and L. Rosen, pp. 356–63, Cambridge and New York: Cambridge University Press.

Ginsburg, Faye, 1987, 'Procreation Stories: Reproduction, Nurturance, and Procreation in Life Narratives of Abortion Activists', *American Ethnologist*, 14, pp. 623–33.

1989, *Contested Lives: The Abortion Debate in an American Community*, Berkeley: University of California Press.

Glazer, Mark, 1982, 'Dowry as Capital Accumulation among the Sephardic Jews of Istanbul, Turkey', in *Jewish Societies in the Middle East*, ed. Sh. Deshen and W. Zenner, pp. 299–309, New York: University Press of America.

Goitein, S. D., 1978, *A Mediterranean Society*, Vol. 3, *The Family*, Berkeley: University of California Press.

Goldberg, Harvey, 1987, 'Torah and Children', in *Judaism Viewed from Within and from Without: Anthropological Studies*, ed. H. Goldberg, pp. 107–30, Albany: State University of New York Press.

Goody, Jack, 1977, 'Mémoire et apprentissage dans les sociétés avec et sans écriture: la transmission du Bagre', *L'Homme*, 17, pp. 29–52.

Gouvernement Général de l'Algérie, 1922, *Tableau général des communes de l'Algérie: situation au 6.3.21*, Algiers: Imprimerie Emile Pfister.

Gudeman, Stephen, and Alberto Rivera, 1990, *Conversations in Colombia: The Domestic Economy in Life and Text*, Cambridge and New York: Cambridge University Press.

Guedj, Max, 1977, *Le voyage en Barbarie*, Paris: Albin Michel.

Les Guides Bleus, 1981, *Algérie*, Paris: Hachette.

Halbwachs, Maurice, 1980, *The Collective Memory*, trans. F. Ditter and V. Y. Ditter, New York: Harper and Row. (First published in French in 1950.)

Halperin, J., and G. Levitte (eds.), 1986, *Mémoire et histoire: actes du XXVème Colloque des Intellectuels Juifs de Langue Française*, Paris: Denoël.

Handler, R., and W. Saxton, 1988, 'Dyssimulation: Reflexivity, Narrative, and the Quest for Authenticity in "Living History"', *Cultural Anthropology*, 3, pp. 242–60.

Herzfeld, Michael, 1985, *The Poetics of Manhood: Contest and Identity in a Cretan Mountain Village*, Princeton: Princeton University Press.

1987, *Anthropology Through the Looking Glass: Critical Ethnography in the Margins of Europe*, Cambridge: Cambridge University Press.

1991a, *A Place in History: Social and Monumental Time in a Cretan Town*, Princeton: Princeton University Press.

1991b, 'Silence, Submission, and Subversion: Toward a Poetic of Womanhood,' in *Contested Identities: Gender and Kinship in Modern Greece*, ed. P. Loizos and E. Papataxiarchis, pp. 79–97, Princeton: Princeton University Press.

Hirschberg, H. Z., 1974–81, *A History of the Jews in North Africa*, 2 vols., Leiden: E. J. Brill.

Hirschon, Renée, 1978, 'Open Body/Closed Space: The Transformation of Female Sexuality', in *Defining Females*, ed. Shirley Ardener, pp. 66–88, London: Croom Helm.

1989, *Heirs of the Greek Catastrophe: The Social Life of Asia Minor Greeks in Piraeus*, New York: Oxford University Press.

Hirschon, Renée, and John Gold, 1982, 'Territoriality and the Home: Environment in a Greek Urban Community', *Anthropological Quarterly*, 55, pp. 63–73.

Jamin, Jean, 1985, 'Le texte ethnographique: argument', *Etudes Rurales*, 97–8, pp. 13–24.

Joutard, Philippe, 1980, 'Un projet régional de recherche sur les ethnotextes', *Annales, E.S.C.*, 35 (1), pp. 176–81.

1983, *Ces voix qui nous viennent du passé*, Paris: Hachette.

Kirshenblatt-Gimblett, Barbara, 1978, 'Culture Shock and Narrative Creativity', in *Folklore in the Modern World*, ed. R. Dorson, pp. 109–22, The Hague and Paris: Mouton.

1987, 'The Folk Culture of Jewish Immigrant Communities: Research Paradigms and Directions', in *The Jews of North America*, ed. M. Rischin, pp. 79–94, Detroit: Wayne State University Press.

1989, 'The Concept and Varieties of Narrative Performance in East European Jewish Culture', in *Explorations in the Ethnography of Speaking*, 2nd edition, ed. R. Bauman and J. Sherzer, pp. 283–308, Cambridge and New York: Cambridge University Press.

Knapp, Steven, 1989, 'Collective Memory and the Actual Past', *Representations*, 26, pp. 123–49.

Kopytoff, Igor, 1986, 'The Cultural Biography of Things: Commoditization as Process', in *The Social Life of Things: Commodities in Cultural Perspective*, ed. A. Appadurai, pp. 64–91, Cambridge and New York: Cambridge University Press.

Kugelmass, Jack, and Jonathan Boyarin, 1983, *From a Ruined Garden: The Memorial Books of Polish Jewry*, New York: Schocken Books.

Laloum, Jean, 1987, 'Sétif la fervente', in *Juifs d'Algérie: images et textes*, ed. Jean Laloum and Jean-Luc Allouche, pp. 154–9, Paris: Editions du Scribe.

Lamaison, Pierre and Elisabeth Claverie, 1982, *L'impossible mariage: violence et parenté en Gévaudan, XVIIème, XVIIIème et XIXème siècles*, Paris: Hachette.

Lapierre, Nicole, 1989, *Le silence de la mémoire: à la recherche des Juifs de Plock*, Paris: Plon.

Le Goff, Jacques, 1986, *Histoire et mémoire*, Paris: Gallimard.

Le Wita, Beatrix, 1984, 'La mémoire familiale des parisiens appartenant aux classes moyennes', *Ethnologie Française*, 14 (1), pp. 57–65.

1985, 'Mémoire: l'avenir du présent', in *Terrain*, 4, pp. 15–26.

1988, *Ni vue ni connue: approche ethnographique de la culture bourgeoise*, Paris: Editions de la Maison des Sciences de l'Homme.

Leibovici, Sarah, 1984, *Chronique des Juifs de Tétouan (1860–1896)*, Paris: Maisonneuve et Larose.

Levi, Giovanni, 1989, 'Les usages de la biographie', *Annales E.S.C.*, 44 (6), pp. 1325–36.

Lévi-Strauss, Claude, 1963, *Structural Anthropology*, vol.1., New York: Basic Books.

1987a, *Anthropology and Myth: Lectures 1951–1982*, Oxford: Blackwell.

1987b, 'De la fidélité au texte', *L'Homme*, 27 (101), pp. 117–39.

1987c, 'La notion de maison', *Terrain*, 9, pp. 34–9.

Lewis, Bernard, 1975, *History Remembered, Recovered, Invented*, Princeton: Princeton University Press.

Lowenthal, David, 1985, *The Past is a Foreign Country*, Cambridge and New York: Cambridge University Press.

Marcus, George E., and Dick Cushman, 1982, 'Ethnographies as Texts', *Annual Review of Anthropology*, 11, pp. 25–69.

Marcus, George, and Michael Fischer, 1986, *Anthropology as Cultural Critique: An Experimental Moment in the Human Sciences*, Chicago: University of Chicago Press.

Martin, Emily, 1987, *The Woman in the Body: A Cultural Analysis of Reproduction*, Boston: Beacon Press.

Maunier, René, 1930, *Mélanges de sociologie nord-africaine*, Paris: Alcan.

La mémoire et l'oubli, 1989, Communications, special issue, no. 49.

Mercier, Ernest, 1903, *Histoire de Constantine*, n.p.: Marle et Biron.

Meyerson, I., 1956, 'Le temps, la mémoire, l'histoire', *Journal de Psychologie Normale et Pathologique*, 3, pp. 333–54.

Mintz, Jerome, 1968, *Legends of the Hasidim*, Chicago: University of Chicago Press.

Moore, Sally, 1987, 'Explaining the Present: Theoretical Dilemmas in Processual Anthropology,' *American Ethnologist*, 14, pp. 727–37.

Morin, Edgar, 1989, *Vidal et les autres*, Paris: Seuil.

Moss, Howard, 1962, *The Magic Lantern of Marcel Proust*, New York: Macmillan.

Munson, Henry, 1984, *The House of Si Abd Allah: The Oral History of a Moroccan Family*, New Haven: Yale University Press.

Myerhoff, Barbara, 1979, *Number Our Days*, New York: Simon and Schuster.

Namer, Gérard, 1987, *Mémoire et société*, Paris: Méridiens-Klincksieck.

Naval Intelligence Division, 1944, *Algeria*, Geographical Handbook Series, Vol. 2, Washington, D.C.: US Government Printing Office.

Netter, G., 1852, 'Les Bahouzim', in *Univers Israélite*, 7, pp. 341–6.

Netting, R., R. Wilk, and E. Arnould (eds.), 1984, *Households: Comparative and Historical Studies of the Domestic Group*, Berkeley: University of California Press.

Nora, Pierre, (ed.) 1986, *Les lieux de mémoire*, Paris: Gallimard.

Nouschi, André, 1961, *Enquête sur le niveau de vie des populations rurales constantinoises de la conquête jusqu'en 1919*, Paris: Presses Universitaires de France.

1980, 'Les villes dans le Maghreb pré-colonial', in *Système urbain et développement au Maghreb*, pp. 37–53, Tunis: Cérès.

Oliver, Paul, 1987, *Dwellings: The House Across the World*, Austin: University of Texas Press.

Orsi, Robert, 1985, *La Madonna of 115th Street: Faith and Community in Italian Harlem (1880–1950)*, New Haven: Yale University Press.

Le Petit Sétifien.

Pezeu-Massabuau, Jacques, 1983, *La maison: espace social*, Paris: Presses Universitaires de France.

Pitkin, Donald S., 1985, *The House that Giacomo Built*, Cambridge and New York: Cambridge University Press.

1990, 'The Domestication of Public Space: Street as Room in Southern Europe', paper presented at the 89th annual meeting of the American Anthropological Association, New Orleans, November 27–December 2.

Pollak, Michael, 1990, *L'expérience concentrationnaire*, Paris: Editions A.-M. Métailié.

Pollak, Michael, and Nathalie Heinich, 1986, 'Le témoignage', *Actes de la Recherche en Sciences Sociales*, 62–3, pp. 3–29.

Rabinow, Paul, 1977, *Reflections on Fieldwork in Morocco*, Berkeley: University of California Press.

1985, 'Fantasia dans la bibliothèque: les représentations sont des faits sociaux, modernité et post-modernité en anthropologie,' *Etudes Rurales*, 97–8, pp. 91–114.

1988, 'Beyond Ethnography: Anthropology as Nominalism,' *Cultural Anthropology*, 3, pp. 355–64.

Raphaël, Freddy, 1980, 'Le travail de la mémoire et les limites de l'histoire orale', *Annales E.S.C.*, 35 (1), pp. 127–145.

Rapoport, A., 1972, *Pour une anthropologie de la maison*, Paris: Dunod.

Rodrigue, Aron, 1989, *De l'instruction à l'émancipation: les enseignants de l'Alliance Israélite Universelle et les Juifs d'Orient, 1860–1939*, Paris: Calmann-Lévy.

Rogers, Susan C., 1975, 'Female Forms of Power and the Myth of Male Dominance: A Model of Female/Male Interaction in Peasant Society', *American Ethnologist*, 2, pp. 727–56.

1991, *Shaping Modern Times in Rural France*, Princeton: Princeton University Press.

Rosen, Lawrence, 1984, *Bargaining for Reality: The Construction of Social Relations in a Muslim Community*, Chicago: University of Chicago Press.

Rubinstein, Katia, 1979, *Mémoire illettrée d'une fillette d'Afrique du Nord à l'époque coloniale*, Paris: Stock.

Ruby, Jay (ed.), 1982, *A Crack in the Mirror, Reflexive Perspectives in Anthropology*, Philadelphia: University of Pennsylvania Press.

Rybczynski, Witold, 1986, *Home: A Short History of an Idea*, New York: Viking.

Sahlins, Marshall, 1981, *Historical Metaphors and Mythical Realities: Structure in the Early History of the Sandwich Islands Kingdom*, Ann Arbor: University of Michigan Press.

Sanson, Henri, 1961, 'L'habitat de la famille en Algérie', *Cahiers Nord-Africains*, 85, pp. 7–23.

Segalen, Martine (ed.), 1989, *L'autre et le semblable*, Paris: Presses du CNRS. *Sétif de l'hexagone,*

Solinas, Piergiorgio, 1986, 'La famille', in *La Méditerranée*, ed. F. Braudel, pp. 81–120, Paris: Flammarion.

Spence, Jonathan, 1984, *The Memory Palace of Matteo Ricci*, New York: Viking Penguin.

Stewart, Kathleen, 1988, 'Nostalgia: A Polemic', *Cultural Anthropology*, 3 (3), pp. 227–41.

Stillman, N., 1989, 'Contacts and Boundaries in the Domain of Language: The Case of Sefriwi Judaeo-Arabic', in *Jews among Arabs: Contacts and Boundaries*, ed. M. Cohen and A. Udovitch, pp. 97–111, Princeton: Darwin Press.

1991, *Jews of Arab Lands in Modern Times*, New York: Jewish Publication Society.

Swearingen, Jan C., 1986, 'Oral Hermeneutics During the Transition to Literacy: The Contemporary Debate', *Cultural Anthropology*, 1 (2), pp. 138–56.

Szyszman, Simon, 1980, *Le Karaïsme: ses doctrines et son histoire*, Lausanne: L'Age d'Homme.

Taylor, Lawrence, 1990, 'On the Power of Rooms,' paper presented at the 89th annual meeting of the American Anthropological Association, New Orleans, November 27–December 2.

Le temps et la mémoire aujourd'hui, 1988, *L'Homme et la Société*, no. 90.

Todorov, Tsvetan, 1981, *Mikhaïl Bakhtine: le principe dialogique*, Paris: Seuil.

Tuan, Yi-Fu, 1974, *Topophilia: A Study of Environmental Perception, Attitudes, and Values*, Englewood Cliffs, N.J.: Prentice-Hall.

Turner, Victor, 1969, *The Ritual Process*, Ithaca: Cornell University Press.

1974, *Fields and Metaphors: Symbolic Action in Human Society*, Ithaca, N.Y.: Cornell University Press.

Udovitch, A., and L. Valensi, 1984, *Juifs en terre d'Islam: les communautés de Djerba*, Paris: Editions des Archives Contemporaines.

United States Army, 1965, *Area Handbook for Algeria*, Washington, D.C.: US Government Printing Office.

1972, *Area Handbook for Algeria*, Washington, D.C.: US Government Printing Office.

Valensi, Lucette, 1986, 'From Sacred History to Historical Memory and Back: The Jewish Past', *History and Anthropology*, 2, pp. 283–305.

Valensi, L., and N. Wachtel, 1991, *Jewish Memories*, Berkeley: University of California Press.

Van Gennep, Arnold, 1914, *En Algérie*, Paris: Mercure de France.

Villanova, Roselyne de, 1989, 'La maison du retour au Portugal', *Annales de la Recherche Urbaine*, 41, pp. 67–75.

Wachtel, Nathan, 1980, 'Le temps du souvenir', *Annales E.S.C.*, 35 (1), pp. 146–8.

1986, 'Remember and Never Forget', *History and Anthropology*, 2, pp. 307–35.

Watson, Laurence, 1976, 'Understanding a Life History as a Subjective Document: Hermeneutical and Phenomenological Perspectives', *Ethos*, 4, pp. 95–131.

Wievorka, A., and I. Niborski, 1983, *Les livres du souvenir: mémoriaux juifs de Pologne*, Paris: Gallimard.

Wolf, Margery, 1968, *The House of Lim: A Study of a Chinese Family Farm*, New York: Appleton-Century-Crofts.

Wylie, Laurence, 1957, *Village in the Vaucluse*, Cambridge, Mass.: Harvard University Press.

Yanagisako, Sylvia Junko, 1979, 'Family and Household: The Analysis of Domestic Groups', *Annual Review of Anthropology*, 8, pp. 161–205.

Yates, Frances, 1966, *The Art of Memory*, Chicago: University of Chicago Press.

Yerushalmi, Hayim Yosef, 1989, *Zakhor: Jewish History and Jewish Memory*, 2nd edition, New York: Schocken Books.

Zenner, Walter, 1965, 'Memorialism: Some Jewish Examples', *American Anthropologist*, 65, pp. 481–3.

Zonabend, Françoise, 1980, *La mémoire longue*, Paris: Presses Universitaires de France.

1985, 'Du texte au prétexte', *Etudes Rurales*, 97–8, pp. 33–8.

Index

Cambridge Studies in Social and Cultural Anthropology

* available in paperback